spaghetti veganese sauce:

heat olive oil. add onion, garlic and chilli, and cook until onion has softened. stir in tomatoes, carrots, tarragon, salt and pepper. simmer for 20 minutes.

see full recipe: day 5, page 37

Laila Madsö

How to be vegan in 28 days

Easy recipes for a healthier life

Change your eating habits for good: veggie guide, easy recipes & vegan weapons

contents

A one-way ticket 6

Vegan, vegetarian, flexitarian, pescatarian . . . 8

How to use this book 11

Cooking principles 14

My favourite ingredients 16

Day 1: You are a vegan already 24

Day 2: Empty your kitchen cabinets 26

Day 3: In all honesty 28

Day 4: Go all in 32

Day 5: Eating out and at work 34

Day 6: Stock up your kitchen with basics 38

Day 7: Food prepping 40

Day 8: Shortcuts and soaking 42

Day 9: Protein and performance 46

Day 10: Satiety and blood sugar 50

Day 11: Feeling good! 52

Day 12: Wheat and convenience food 56

Day 13: Health check and supplements 60

Day 14: New cooking skills 62

Day 15: Omega 3 and algae 64

Day 16: Flavour, fermenting and umami craving 66

Day 17: A new food culture + food waste 68

Day 18: Beyond Meat burger, anyone? 70

Day 19: The domino effect 72

Day 20: Celebrity vegans 74

Day 21: Flex that culinary muscle 76

Day 22: A true friend 78

Day 23: Vegan on a budget 80

Day 24: Travelling and on the go 82

Day 25: For the men 84

Day 26: Pep-talk and one final push 86

Day 27: Are you cheating? 88

Day 28: Completed & let's celebrate! 90

17 hearty dinners

Cauliflower risotto with capers, herb oil and raw marinated cauliflower 96

Cauliflower rice with quinoa, tomatoes, crispy seeds and hummus 98

Whole roasted cauliflower with chipotle, cashew nuts and pea purée 100

Roasted butternut squash with quinoa, kale and crispy pumpkin seeds 104

Red Thai curry with butternut squash, coconut milk, lime and wild rice 106

Cabbage salad with fennel, mango, pomegranate and fried quinoa 110

Grilled cabbage with miso dressing, pea purée, sunflower seeds and sprouts 112

Broccoli and avocado wok with caramelised onion hummus, chilli and sprouts 116

Tenderstem broccoli and tofu in black bean
  sauce with cherry tomatoes and
  sesame seeds   118
Celeriac steaks with crushed edamame,
  mushrooms and sriracha dressing   122
Salt-baked and grilled sweet potato
  with romaine lettuce, wild rice and
  walnuts   126
Tacos with five-spice fried sweet potato,
  avocado cream, pickled red onions
  and mango salsa   128
Red lentil dhal with cumin, radishes,
  edamame and horseradish   132
Falafel with pickled onions and
  coconut yoghurt   134
Garlic-roasted chickpeas and carrots
  with tahini dressing and herb quinoa 138
Salt-baked beets with beetroot hummus,
  chickpeas, spinach and hazelnuts   140
Fried rice with edamame, mushrooms
  and carrots   142

23 vegan weapons

Classic vinaigrette   146
French mustard vinaigrette   147
Balsamic vinaigrette   147
Green herb oil   147
Vegan pesto   149
Five-spice   149
Classic hummus   151
Beetroot hummus   151
Caramelised red onion hummus   151
Pea hummus   151
Red cabbage and apple slaw   152

Pea purée with hot chilli   153
Grilled aubergine purée   155
Pickled red onions   155
Vegan mayonnaise   157
Vegan aioli   157
Sriracha dressing   157
Tahini dressing   159
Miso dressing   159
Mustard dressing   159
Crispy chipotle cashew nuts   161
Turmeric-roasted peanuts   161
Fennel-roasted chickpeas   161

Diary notes   162
Index   166
Thanks   169
Testimonials from previous meat eaters 170

a one-way ticket

Now you're on to something! It started at the very moment you laid your hands on this book. People have their reasons for giving up meat and animal products. And you have yours. Maybe you've started to recognise the zeitgeist; you've begun to connect the dots between health, the environment, food, climate and animal rights, and discovered a new complexity that you didn't see before. You now see things holistically. Maybe you're worried about the climate and environmental emissions. Or maybe the ethical dilemma of animal welfare is your biggest concern. One thing is for sure: we often hear about the health benefits of eating vegetables in the media.

It doesn't really matter why you want to do a 28-day vegan challenge. I will teach you how to do it. Over the course of the next month you will, most likely, eat way more veggies, and a lot less meat, than ever before.

This book shows you all you need to know to thrive on a colourful, tasty and nutritious plant-based diet.

Over the next four weeks, you will establish new routines, expand your taste buds and gain knowledge that will be at your service for the rest of your life. To eat 100 per cent plant-based is easier than you might think; however, it does require focus and dedication. At least in the beginning. It takes somewhere between three and six weeks to change a habit. To change the way you think about food may take longer. Nonetheless, you have taken your first step. You have shown up at the start line with an intention to change your diet, and that's an excellent opportunity for new eating habits that last. Soon you will find that your new food experiences will stick with you. Just imagine, your old scratching-your-head-lacking-in-dinner-ideas will soon be a vague memory. In fact, before you know it you will have become a vegan guru shaking out delicious plant-based meals with no recipe whatsoever!

Meanwhile, we'll seize the opportunity to clean out a few misconceptions about plant-based living. This book lets people ease their way into it with their hands in their pockets and an open mind. You'll find that life as a vegan is stress-less, full of energy and filled with fun kitchen stories.

Over the next month, you'll be guided towards a healthier and more conscious relationship with food. You'll be urged to regularly check the contents of your fridge and kitchen cabinets, and you'll be advised to follow simple step-by-step instructions and basic cooking principles, all of which will make vegetables the easy choice for your dinner plate.

A daily reminder will make you more aware of the link between food and your wellbeing, which will reinforce your new eating habits. You will notice a positive effect on both your body and mind.

New and old theories of nutrition point in the same direction: you are what you eat. By following the eating plan in this book, all you risk is ending up eating a lot of veggies for a few weeks. The likelihood of you feeling happier and full of energy is greater, too. There is also a major possibility you will find yourself glowing with more radiant skin and a lighter mind. If you are among those who would welcome a few less kilos around your waist, such results are probable, as well as less pain in your knees and shoulders, better sleep, better digestion and more balanced blood sugar. In fact, there is a great chance that in 28 days, you will be left with an abundance of life force and vitality.

Chances are you will happily continue eating more veggies and plant-based food even after your meatless month is over. All the medical doctors in the world will cheer you on and applaud such a healthy outcome.

now you're on to something!

vegan, vegetarian, flexitarian, pescatarian . . .

Now that you are about to start 28 days as a vegan, let's have a look at some key terms. No one likes to be pigeonholed, and people approach veganism or vegetarianism differently. However, there are a few labels worth noting.

Vegans eat only plant-based foods and no animal products. In addition to vegetables, vegans eat beans, legumes, grains, nuts, seeds, berries, oils, herbs and fruit. Vegans don't eat meat, fish, eggs, honey or dairy products like butter, milk and cheese. Some people take their vegan ethical stance further and say no to leather goods, all clothing containing animal by-products like wool from sheep, and commercial beauty products, to avoid all forms of animal exploitation. The important thing is that you find a way to facilitate change. Being vegan is your personal journey to something bigger than you, and it will increase the demand for plant-based alternatives that are better for both people and the planet. You could say that turning vegan is one small step for you, one giant leap for humankind. Remember, there is no vegan police that will come to arrest you if you do something 'wrong' like wear leather shoes or use up your old moisturiser. Most vegans do not live a 100 per cent vegan lifestyle, and in this book, being vegan is all about food.

Vegetarians, like vegans, do not eat meat or any ingredients that cause animals to be slaughtered. However, they do include eggs, cheese and dairy products in their diet. Many people find it easier to be vegetarian than vegan. In fact, cheese is said to be the number one reason more vegetarians aren't going vegan!

Flexitarian, a relatively new word, incorporates the idea of a flexible approach to eating. A flexitarian has a primarily vegetarian diet, but incorporates meat and animal products like dairy, eggs and even seafood occasionally. Flexitarians more often choose plant-based options over animal foods. The popular concept of Meatless Mondays has undoubtedly encouraged a lot of people to give up meat, fish, dairy and eggs more often. What if #meatlessmonth becomes the new #meatlessmonday!?

Pescatarian Someone who never eats meat, but includes fish, eggs and dairy products in their diet.

In addition, there are a few more terms you may, or may not, have stumbled upon here or there:

Lacto-vegetarian A vegetarian who consumes milk and dairy products, but no meat, fish or eggs.

Ovo-vegetarian Someone who doesn't eat meat, dairy or fish, but does include eggs in their diet.

Ovo-lacto-vegetarian A vegetarian who consumes some animal products, like eggs and dairy. Unlike pescatarians they do not eat fish or seafood.

Oh, lordy, you say. Does it really have to be so particular? Absolutely not! No matter how you choose to label yourself — or not — the all-important thing is that you have taken the first step towards a plant-based diet. Where you land further on is yet unknown. Changing eating habits is a process that takes dedication over time.

We all love cheese! So did I. I used to have a real affection for Brie, Parmesan, Stilton and Roquefort. Until one day I decided to end my relationship with cheese. I've never looked back, and now I enjoy the many vegan cheese alternatives instead. No problem.

how to eat satisfying wholefoods

how to use this book

this is not a cookbook.

Actually, I made it a point that you shouldn't have to read many recipes over the next few weeks. I'd rather teach you simple skills to turn vegetables into delicious food. You are going to prepare vegan meals out of not only vegetables, but also beans, lentils and seeds. Home-cooked food and no ready-made substitutes. No need to worry about becoming a vegan junkie full of refined carbs, cornflour and too many soy products. You can jump directly to Day 12 to learn more about how vegan convenience food can be a health trap.

This book shows you how to eat satisfying wholefoods and easy-to-make dinners that taste amazing. You will learn cooking techniques and principles that make many different meals out of one single vegetable. Take cauliflower as an example. Soon, you'll see this hero ingredient for what it's really worth — shining like a star in cauliflower risotto; covered with mustard vinaigrette and roasted whole; sliced, fried and dressed with chipotle mayo; or as a hearty sidekick to a creamy dhal.

Even if this 28-day plan is more about how-to methods than about recipes, it's still useful to have some key recipes up your sleeve. That's why you'll get my vegan weapons: 23 simple yet tasty protein-rich sides, as well as sauces and dressings made of olive oil and other fats that are good for you. All perfectly balanced with salty, sweet and sour tastes, these sidekicks are big on flavour and nutrient value. You will find that these vegan weapons become your new favourites, and you will continue to use them for the rest of your life, regardless of which direction your diet takes after your meatless month is over.

In addition to this, I have provided 17 hearty dinner recipes to combine with the 23 weapons. These dishes are all made from common vegetables you'll already know, but now you'll be inspired to try them in different ways. Together these recipes will provide you with a brilliant starting point on your plant-based journey.

The aim of this book is not to transform you into anything — not even a vegan. If you take anything away from it, I hope it's that you start to eat less meat, a little more wild-caught fish, and mostly greens and veggies — which is exactly what I think both you and I hoped for.

Omega 3

To some people fish is the epitome of healthy food. How, then, could a diet without fish and seafood be good for you? The answer is, yes, fish can be healthy. Salmon and other kinds of fish rich in omega-3 fatty acids play an important role in a Western diet. However, new studies show that the fish we eat nowadays isn't as rich in omega 3 as it used to be, and unfortunately that counts for the popular farmed salmon as well. The depletion is mostly due to the manufactured feed used in fish farming. Omega 3 in the form of a fish oil supplement is an excellent choice for everyone, and although fish isn't included in my vegan diet, I still choose to add fish oil. Omega-3 fatty acids are also found in canola oil and flaxseed oil; however, plant-based omega 3 (ALA) doesn't convert easily into EPA and DHA, which are the types of omega 3 found in fish — and it's EPA and DHA that have the many health benefits. If you are pregnant or nursing, you should always consider a fish oil supplement. You could also choose a seaweed and algae supplement, as this is where the fish get their omega 3. Jump to Day 15 to learn more on this. Also note that although fish can be an important source of selenium, you will find this powerful mineral in selenium-rich plant-based foods like legumes, lentils and brazil nuts as well.

You will learn everything you need to know about supplements like vitamin B12, iodine and vitamin D in the next four weeks.

Weight control and stress management

One major health benefit of a plant-based diet is stable blood sugar. That means not only an improved mood and better energy, but you will also feel satisfied for longer after your meals. Stay away from refined carbs like sugary foods and wheat-based convenience foods, and stick to the plan in this book, and your energy levels will hit new highs throughout the day without the need to fuel up on snacks in between meals. Four weeks of skipping all meat and dairy products will also mean that you'll eat less saturated fat, which is typically found in animal-based foods.

A key element of the plan in this book is to learn how to be content eating only plant-based foods while at the same time avoiding sugary convenience foods and refined grains. Day by day you are encouraged to reduce your consumption of wheat and introduce spelt and different kinds of gluten-free grains. All these steps combined will help you either lose weight or keep you at your ideal weight — and all the while you will be eating hearty food and never skipping a meal. Actually, a common side effect of the 28-day plan in this book is weight loss. Many people have lost several kilos without even making an effort to do so. Imagine what could happen when you put extra effort into it!

Your mental health is also related to what you eat. New research shows that the global increase in mental health problems is associated with Western food and lifestyle. Plant-based diets encourage a richer variety of gut bacteria, which in turn contributes to better brain function. Research shows that increased intake of vegetables, oats, wild rice, nuts, seeds and fruits can reduce mood swings. For many, it is not uncommon to eat comfort food when feeling depressed. Filling the plate with plant foods can help feed two birds with one scone: reducing weight and improving mood.

If your goal is to get in better shape and lose weight, it is advisable that you hold yourself accountable and write down everything you eat, as well as how you feel throughout this month. Making a habit of noting food and mood in a diary or in the diary notes section in the back of this book (see page 162) every evening makes it easier to see the connections – and the results.

cooking principles

With the help of this book, you will learn some simple ways to cook nourishing meals without following a recipe. So, it's about understanding how to combine simple ingredients and make them into a complete meal.

An important element is to make food that is healthy and satisfying but that tastes good, too. Very good. Over the next four weeks the goal is to discover a new-found delight in food and the sanctuary of your kitchen. You will learn how to cook and eat more vegetables every day, and how to cook freestyle with or without the need for recipes. You will find more enjoyment in cooking than you ever did before, which will last for the rest of your life.

You'll come a long way without the need for recipes if you can master some simple cooking principles. First and foremost, it is about the right balance between the following basic tastes:

Sweet
Salty
Sour
Bitter
Umami

A good example is how the sour taste is balanced by the sweet in homemade lemonade. Lemonade is made from tart lemons that get softer in taste when we add sugar. The result is a well-balanced and deliciously refreshing drink. Lemonade is full of sugar, so this is meant as an example, not a daily recommendation. Many Asian sauces are based on the same principle, where the sour is neutralised by sugar to achieve a very tasty result.

Making uncomplicated dishes with vegetables without a recipe is like cracking a code, and once you've cracked it, there's no limit to what you can make.

There are some simple rules for how to balance the different flavours, and in this book you will learn smart techniques that let your vegetable bowls burst with delicious tastes. Homemade, plant-based and balanced out with a little salt, olive oil and lemon – this way of cooking is both easy and fun. Why don't you involve the whole family and give names to the dishes you cook together? Voilà, you get a personal menu of family favourites.

When cooking with vegetables, it is good to know how to balance the sour and the bitter in the ingredients. Sour and bitter are prominent flavours in many vegetables. If you make a salad, adding a simple vinaigrette made from olive oil, mustard and maple syrup will balance these out. Simply put, the oil and sweetness will reduce the bitter and sour flavours.

Similarly, salt will remove some of the bitterness in plants. If you add a pinch of salt to a salad with a lemon and oil vinaigrette, the salt reduces the bitterness and acts as a flavour enhancer.

By following the simple steps and learning the basic cooking principles in this book, you will find that your vegan journey goes smoothly. What you do on day 29 is entirely up to you, but I bet you won't regret your 28 days as a vegan.

My meals are often tapas-style with many different light dishes on the table, and always with dips or other satisfying sides.

Alexander Berg, one of the top chefs in Norway, former captain of the Norwegian national cooking team and former head of the Norwegian Culinary Institute, quickly grasped my way of thinking, and the dishes in this book have been developed in collaboration with him.

Alexander's three keys to succeeding with vegetable dishes in his own words:

1 My best advice for making plant-based food is to use vegetables and ingredients you already know and like. Unlike when I cook with fish or meat, when these play a natural starring role, I start by selecting a vegetable for the leading role, one that will serve as the substantial main ingredient, and build the dish around it.

2 Don't be afraid of salt. It's my favourite flavour enhancer. Of course, no one likes their food too salty but salt brings out the natural flavour in vegetables and reduces the bitterness that many vegetables naturally have in them.

3 Try experimenting with broccoli. It's incredibly versatile. It's probably my favourite vegetable. I like to eat it raw and marinated or cooked lightly with chilli flakes, garlic, salt and lemon.

my favourite ingredients

The foods in this list have been selected because they are very useful to kick-start your 28 days of being vegan. This will be your go-to ingredients list when cooking at home. All these wholefoods are nutritious and contribute to a healthy and balanced diet – and they are easy to combine. Feel free to use organic vegetables, and wash or scrub all produce to get rid of soil, microbes and pesticides. Know that even organic vegetables can become contaminated with pesticides. Often you don't have to peel vegetables as long as you wash them.

Onions and red onions True superfoods that are high in dietary fibre and antioxidants, as well as having many other healthy properties. Onions in all varieties give juice and power to your cooking. Alternate or combine red and yellow onions and shallots, and use them raw or fried. In the onion family there are also spring onions, leeks and chives, which all contribute to taste.

Carrots Rich in orange-red beta-carotene, which the body converts to vitamin A. Good for the immune system and skin. Lightly cooked carrots are more nutritious, but you still get plenty of nutrients, such as carotenoids, from raw carrots.

Sweet potatoes Rich in beta-carotene and calcium, and they contain slower-release carbohydrates than regular white potatoes, which means they don't spike your blood sugar or insulin to the same extent. Use in the same way as regular potatoes.

Avocados Contain a lot of healthy monounsaturated fat and vitamin E. Avocado helps the body absorb fat-soluble nutrients from other ingredients, such as lycopene from tomatoes. The nutrients in avocados help to strengthen the immune system and balance hormones. Spread it on toast or use in salads. Try it as a topping on a quinoa dish.

Beetroots Lower blood pressure, and contain fibre which can enhance good gut bacteria and digestion. They also contain iron and nitrates which can improve your physical performance and cut your risk of heart disease. Sweet in taste. Pan-fry or bake on a bed of salt, or roast in the oven with other vegetables. Try cutting into raw carpaccio-thin slices or lightly steam and mix into a green salad.

Tomatoes and cherry tomatoes Contain plenty of the important phytonutrient lycopene, vitamin C and fibre. Lightly cooking tomatoes increases the availability of lycopene, which has many health benefits. You can drizzle tomatoes with olive oil and add a tiny pinch of salt, and enjoy them in any way you prefer. Tomatoes are among the most useful vegetables around. Excellent for roasting or chopped in a tomato-based sauce. You can also use tinned chopped tomatoes or tomato paste.

Spinach Full of beta-carotene, which is converted to vitamin A, calcium, which strengthens bones, and vitamin C, which is good for skin and hair. Spinach also contains a lot of iron, but is not considered a good source of iron because of the oxalic acid that prevents it from being easily absorbed into the body. However, spinach contains so much vitamin C that it increases the absorption of iron from other foods. Sauté, stir-fry or blend into dishes.

Broccoli One of the most nutritious vegetables you can eat! High levels of vitamin C and K, folate, beta carotene, cancer-preventing sulforaphane, calcium and potassium. Keep optimal nutrient levels by steaming or sautéing instead of boiling.

Lemon High in vitamin C. Lemon has an acidic pH, but once metabolised it has an alkaline effect, which in turn helps balance the acid–alkaline ratio in the body. Lemon juice is used in cooking to provide freshness, flavour and acidity. Starting off your day with a glass of water mixed with the juice of half a lemon may contribute to a healthy immune system and promote weight loss and better digestion.

Celeriac Rich in folate, vitamin C, potassium, manganese and copper. Salt-bake it in the oven, which takes less than an hour. Also good as root mash: cut into cubes and cook with carrots and sweet potato. Pour off the water and mash with some oat milk, salt and pepper.

Garlic More than just a spice, raw garlic helps strengthen the immune system and can prevent typical lifestyle diseases. Garlic is considered to be blood thinning and contains plenty of B vitamins as well as vitamins A and C. Cut garlic cloves into slices and lightly toast in a pan or bake whole cloves in the oven at 180°C/160°C fan/gas mark 4 for 10 minutes, which brings out the sweetness and depth in contrast to the sharp taste of raw garlic. The nutrient content is slightly impaired by high heat. I use both raw and cooked garlic in many dishes, often in dressings, and always in hummus. By the way, did you know that eating parsley or apple can alleviate 'garlic breath'?

Red peppers Full of vitamin C – in fact, up to three times more vitamin C than oranges. Cut into strips and pan-fry, or slice in half and roast in the oven. Eat raw in salads and mix with mango for a mango salsa.

All the food we eat and digest has either an acidic or alkaline effect in the body. Vegetables help increase alkalinity. Meat, dairy and fish are acidic. For optimal health you want more alkalinity and less acidity. Therefore, it is good to avoid too many acid-promoting foods, such as meat, sugar, processed foods, dairy and grains.

Pumpkin Has a high vitamin A and potassium content. Use in the same way as sweet potato and squash (pumpkin is, in fact, a type of squash). Perhaps the bright bottle pumpkin is most common, but the Japanese Hokkaido pumpkin is also sometimes available. Pumpkin can be cooked, fried, baked or pickled. Don't be intimidated by its size; divide the pumpkin in half and peel with a large kitchen knife.

Kale Full of vitamins and antioxidants. It's a close relative of broccoli, Brussels sprouts, cauliflower and good old cabbage. Rich in iron and calcium. Cut off the stems and massage the green leaves with a drizzle of olive oil and a pinch of salt until they are moistened by the liquid released. Some people prefer to cook it. Try pan-frying coarsely chopped kale with a splash of water and a pinch of salt until just wilted. Pour off the liquid and squeeze over the juice of half a lemon. Season to taste with pepper and a drizzle of olive oil.

Herbs I use herbs both for taste and for decoration. A generous sprinkle of fresh herbs over your dishes not only looks delicious, it will also benefit your health because herbs contain plenty of natural plant chemicals like antioxidants, phytonutrients and essential oils.

Sprouts Powerful and nutrient-dense little plants that you can use to top off literally any dish. In addition to adding flavour, a sprinkle of fresh green sprouts always makes a plate look tasty. The actual germination process is initiated as a seed comes into contact with water: it begins to swell and eventually the little tip appears. Sprouts can be used raw, gently heated or pan-fried. Feel free to drizzle extra virgin olive oil over sprouts for even better nutrient absorption. You can eat any sprouts that come from edible plants.

The most common herbs are:
basil
coriander
dill
mint
parsley
rosemary
sage
thyme

Common sprouts are:
alfalfa
cress
mung bean
broccoli
radish
red clover
sunflower
chickpeas

Dry foods

Fresh vegetables are one thing. Other important components of a plant-based diet are protein-rich and mineral-rich legumes (lentils, beans, peas), which many plant eaters eat — in one form or another — several times a week. These satisfying legumes also have a low glycaemic index. That is, they are digested slowly and stabilise blood sugar. If you buy dry legumes such as beans, lentils, chickpeas and soya beans in bulk, you'll save money. And soon you'll have installed the good habit of soaking your legumes the night before (see Day 8 for more on soaking). Tinned legumes have already been cooked, so are a great option if you don't have time to soak, although they do work out more expensive. For better digestion and less bloating, remember to drink a glass of water when eating beans and high-fibre seeds.

Beans Rich in B vitamins, iron, calcium, zinc and magnesium. I usually use butter beans, kidney beans, pinto beans and black beans.

Chickpeas Protein-rich, high in folate, iron, manganese and magnesium. They're usable in all vegetable dishes. They are cholesterol-lowering, they stabilise blood sugar and act as a prebiotic in the gut. Combining chickpeas with turmeric and garlic will increase the health benefits. How perfect, then, that all these ingredients make a delicious hummus!

Lentils Beans, lentils and peas are inexpensive and nutritious superfoods and have lots in common when it comes to health benefits. Good for digestion and preventive for heart disease. Use lentils in dhal and soups, or mix with quinoa for a hearty lentil salad.

Quinoa One of the most nutritious grains, which contains all the essential amino acids. Provides an extra protein boost if you work out a lot. Available as red and white small seeds, and makes a perfect mix with lentils and beans. Best served as a main course mixed with vegetables and a dressing, rather than as a side. It's a healthier substitute for rice due to its higher protein and fibre content. Quinoa can also be made into flakes and flour, and various foods like pasta and bread.

Rice Replace refined white rice with wholegrain brown rice or wild rice; both are full of vibrant health and have a delicious nutty taste.

Soaking
Give dry beans and chickpeas in bulk a chance! I'll teach you how to soak them on Day 8 (see page 42). Jump ahead and take a sneak peek if you want to start soaking today!

Wholegrain rice is a source of healthy carbohydrates and fibre, zinc and B vitamins. Wholegrain rice or brown rice means that the rice is unpolished and has the shell intact. Wild rice is my favourite rice; it's nourishing and offers a variety of nutrients, and is much better for you than refined white rice. Wild rice is, in fact, categorised as a grass and is almost black in colour with a hazelnut-like flavour. Wild rice must be soaked, but it is worth the time because it contains more protein, more iron and more B vitamins than all other types of rice.

Oats Full of fibre and naturally gluten free. Due to contamination from other cereals in agricultural production, it is important that you buy certified gluten-free oats if you have coeliac disease. Buy rolled oats or steel-cut oats, which are less processed than 'instant' oats.

Seeds and nuts

Seeds and nuts contain vitamins, minerals, protein, fibre and healthy unsaturated fats. I often use different seeds and nuts interchangeably. Toast them in a pan or roast them in the oven at 180°C/160°C fan/gas mark 4 for 5–10 minutes. Sprinkle them on salads, soups and dinners for crunch and taste. A small handful of nuts works well as a quick energy boost.

Chia seeds Rich in essential fatty acids (omega 3 and omega 6), fibre, minerals and even protein. They expand ten times in size when added to liquid. Popular in porridge and smoothies. Can be used as a substitute for eggs. To replace 1 egg, mix 1 tablespoon of crushed chia seeds with 3 tablespoons of water. After 5–10 minutes, you end up with a gel that can be used in place of the egg in recipes.

Flaxseeds High in fibre and omega-3 fatty acids. Use a pestle and mortar to crush the flaxseeds before eating them. Crushed flaxseeds have the best nutrient absorption and can also be used as a substitute for eggs in pastries. Mix 1 tablespoon of crushed flaxseeds with 3 tablespoons of water and leave for 5 minutes until the mixture thickens and becomes gel-like. For better digestion and less bloating, remember to drink water when eating flaxseeds and other high-fibre foods.

These are the nuts I use most often:
almonds
cashew nuts
walnuts
peanuts
brazil nuts

Pumpkin seeds Rich in protein, vitamin E and the minerals potassium, magnesium, zinc and iron. Lightly pan-fry and use as a topping on porridge, bread and salads.

Sesame seeds Rich in the amino acid tryptophan, calcium, vitamin E, magnesium and iron. Fry them and use as a topping on porridge, soups and salads. Also try tahini, which is a paste made from crushed sesame seeds and one of the main ingredients in hummus, see page 151.

Sunflower seeds A good source of protein, but it is advisable to limit the use of sunflower seeds because they contain the heavy metal cadmium that can damage the kidneys. Sunflower oil has a lower level of cadmium than raw seeds. Pan-fried sunflower seeds are a healthy and delicious snack, but remember to eat in moderation.

Spices

Spices play an important role in plant-based cooking. They're a flavour enhancer and also provide health benefits. Be generous with spices and notice how your food changes in both taste and colour depending on which you use.

Salt is not really a spice, but a flavour enhancer that we discussed in the chapter on cooking principles.

Basic ingredients that are nice to have

Aquafaba This word sounds more mysterious than it is. Aquafaba is the water or brine in a tin of beans or chickpeas. Use it instead of egg white in plant-based cooking, including baking. Make it a habit to save the liquid every time you open a tin of chickpeas or beans, but be aware that the water varies depending on which type of beans you use. Look for the brine that is on the thicker side with a consistency similar to egg whites. If the aquafaba is too watery, you can reduce the liquid by cooking gently in a pan. Cool it before use. Aquafaba keeps in the fridge for five days when stored in an airtight container.

My most frequently used spices:
pepper
cumin
ginger
cinnamon
turmeric
cayenne pepper

Apple cider vinegar, red wine vinegar or white wine vinegar balance and enhance the taste of vegetables. Use sparingly but frequently in all plant-based cooking. Look for organic brands.

Coconut oil can replace butter when frying and baking.

Coconut milk can replace single cream in most dishes.

Miso Flavour enhancer that gives the anticipated and distinctly sweet-filled umami flavour to sauces, dressings and toppings — for example, on roasted cauliflower.

Nutritional yeast Not the same as regular yeast! This is an inactive yeast that tastes cheesy and provides a nutritious depth to dishes where you would otherwise use Parmesan or other hard cheese.

Olive oil The most commonly used ingredient in the Mediterranean diet — and the vegan diet. Choose cold-pressed extra virgin oil for vinaigrette and dressings. It tastes better and has more antioxidants and nutrients than standard olive oil, which is good for cooking and pan-frying.

Rapeseed oil can be used for salad dressings, as well as for frying and baking. Look for local producers, and always choose glass bottles and store it in a dark place. I do use rapeseed oil to cook, but I use it sparingly as it is often highly processed. Remember that you should not generally use high-quality extra virgin oil for frying, as it's expensive and frying can impact its flavour. Use it for cold dishes and salads, and for making pesto or hummus.

Tahini B-vitamin-rich sticky paste made from sesame seeds that gives the umami flavour to hummus and dressings.

Tamari / soy sauce A flavour enhancer that gives a saltier and smokier umami flavour than miso.

you are a vegan already

Is a vegan diet satisfying? Do you need a piece of meat or salmon for dinner to be a 'proper' dinner? Are you struggling to find plant-based ingredients at the supermarket? Are you unsure of what to put on the plate and end up with potatoes, gravy, a salad leaf and an empty void where the piece of meat used to be?

The first thing most people wonder when considering a vegan diet is this: what can I eat? And will I be satisfied? Somehow, there is the idea that vegans live on foods that taste like cardboard and boring, bland salads of cucumber, tomato slices, corn and lettuce.

Nothing can be further from the truth.

A vegan's kitchen cabinet?

If you take a look in the kitchen cabinets of any meat eater, it's likely you will find a variety of plant-based foods. These are products without any meat or dairy content: peanut butter, most types of margarine, yeast, beans, bread, tinned tomatoes, cereals, fresh herbs such as basil and parsley, dried spices, ketchup, jam and marmalade, olive oil, soy sauce, mustard, coconut milk, coffee, crackers, raisins, flour, tomato juice, nuts and, of course, fruits and vegetables – tinned, fresh or frozen.

All this is vegan. And these are the foods you will need for your daily vegan menu.

Tips for the first seven days

Skip cereal with cow's milk for breakfast, and eat overnight oats with a dollop of oat crème fraîche and berries instead. Voilà, you're in! So, you already eat a lot of plant-based food. It's just that you haven't cut out meat from your diet. Yet.

today's task

Here's your first task for your first day as a vegan: take stock of your cupboards! Look for plant-based food in your kitchen cabinets and fridge to get an overview of what you're already eating that is vegan. Take out all tins and packets and write a complete food inventory. Continue tomorrow if you have to. This gives you a head start now that you are about to begin shopping for a plant-based diet.

When you finish sorting out the kitchen, you will see that you have a plethora of plant-based foods and products in your home. You have a vegan starter kit without having made a single new purchase.

You are already in action!

Now it's easy for you to move on. All you have to do is make a soft start and use what you have already. Try out some new dishes and repeat over the next couple of days.

As mentioned before, this book gives you the keys to making satisfying meals based on basic cooking principles instead of recipes. It's all about understanding how vegetables can turn into a delicious balanced meal.

For example, make a simple dinner of fried beans or lentils and place half an avocado on top. Drizzle over a good olive oil and season with salt and pepper and a sprinkle of fresh herbs.

Slice an avocado and spread on two slices of bread made of spelt. Spice it up with cayenne pepper, sea salt and a few drops of olive oil.

Cook brown rice, top it with broccoli and hummus and drizzle over a teaspoon of olive oil and a few drops of balsamic vinegar.

Replace the cow's milk in your pancake batter with oat milk, which often is more sustainable than water-craving almonds used for almond milk, and always a more sustainable choice than cow's milk.

ps.

Remember to mark in your diary that this is Day 1, and make a mark for the next 28 days ahead.

empty your kitchen cabinets

Now that you have created a complete inventory of your kitchen cabinets, your next task is to be a touch more systematic about it.

If you found oats in the cupboard, and it has been a long time since you've eaten porridge, now is the time. Pimp up your porridge by cooking it with pieces of apple and a sprinkle of cinnamon. Or better yet: did you find chia seeds? Then add a tablespoon of chia seeds along with the oats. They create a delicious pudding-like texture — not to mention that these tiny little seeds are packed with protein and essential nutrients, such as omega-3 fatty acids, antioxidants and fibre.

Don't like porridge? Then try something else. Having oat milk in your cup of coffee or pouring it over your cereal are easy ways to transition from cow's milk. Oats are often more sustainable than almonds. Oat milk is just as creamy as the cow's milk you are used to. Perfect for coffee. There are also several other types of oat products, as well as coconut milk, which can replace cream and crème fraîche in cooking.

Day 2 is all about looking at your food with new eyes. What did you find at the back of your fridge that you really like? Keep eating these foods — yes, eat them at least once a week. Twice a week. Maybe three. The idea is that if you have a few tins of chopped tomatoes, there are many options for how to prepare them: make tomato soup one day, chilli sin carne with beans and lentils another day, and this weekend make spaghetti veganese — the vegan version of the family favourite everyone knows as Bolognese.

the point in eating plant-based is to learn to redo vegetables for a meal.

today's task

Divide a sheet of paper into four columns. At the top of these columns write the headings: Breakfast, Lunch, Dinner, Snacks/Emergency.

Today, on your second day as a vegan, use your food inventory from Day 1 and write down the foods in the column that you think they are most suited to; that is, when you think you most want to eat them.

Now, start cooking using these foods. Relax, loosen up and enjoy practising your culinary skills. Do you fancy spaghetti Bolognese? Well, now make it completely meatless. Later, I'll give you a simple recipe for tomato sauce that is great for a quick-fix dinner.

Have you tried the new varieties of veggie pasta available? I don't eat spaghetti very often, instead I use pasta made of beans, lentils, buckwheat and sweet potato, to name a few. If you know that eating wheat makes you feel slightly heavy afterwards, I recommend testing out some of these types instead of regular wheat pasta.

Don't fancy pasta? Then choose anything else – just reach your hand into the cupboard and take out the first thing you touch. Use this as a main ingredient and pour it into the frying pan or empty it into a saucepan. Compose and be creative. Chop up some onion and crush a garlic clove and put it all in the frying pan. Who cares if it doesn't look like something you've seen before! The point here is to explore how you can turn vegetables into a tasty meal.

Again, it's not about following recipes, but more about looking at vegetables with new eyes and starting to use them as the main event in your dishes.

So far you haven't made one single purchase for your new vegan diet. Tomorrow, however, you're going shopping.

a few words about soy and soy drinks

Soy is a complete vegetable protein, and a popular plant substitute for meat and dairy products. There is some disagreement about whether soy is healthy or not. This is partly due to the fact that soy contains oestrogen like compounds called isoflavones, which have the same structure as the female hormone oestrogen. Such oestrogens are found in several vegetables, not just soy, and there is ongoing research to refute that plant oestrogen affects us in the same way as the female hormone oestrogen. In this book I consider it okay to eat a moderate amount of whole or unrefined soy foods like edamame, tofu and miso a couple of times a week. That's why you'll find these in the recipes further ahead. It is worth mentioning that fermented soy products such as miso and tempeh are easier to digest than processed soy. Highly processed 'soy protein isolate', often found in plant-based ready-to-eat vegan burgers and vegetarian products, contains a higher and more concentrated amount of isoflavones — and protein — than the natural raw material. That is why I recommend using whole, unrefined soy foods.

in all honesty

The first ten days as a vegan are a little challenging.

You have to figure out what to buy and what to make for dinner. You will examine ingredients and spend longer at the supermarket. This is partly because you are no longer acting on autopilot, filling your shopping basket with all the usual stuff. Now instead you are looking around for new and for the most part unknown foods you have never laid eyes on before. At the same time, you will find that you become one of those people who hang around the shelves carefully reading the product labels. This is going to be the new you, at least for the next couple of weeks. And you'll be surprised to see that you have consumed a variety of ingredients and products that you really have no idea what they are or what they contain.

In the beginning, the most important thing is to keep it simple: check to see if the food contains any animal ingredients such as milk, cream and cheese. You will see ingredients such as rennin, casein (milk protein), egg yolk powder, lysozyme, albumin, aspic, gelatin, honey (many do not know that honey does not belong to a vegan diet), dry milk, whey protein and whey. It's pretty obvious that some of these come from animals, but several ingredients are probably unknown to most people, and you have no idea what they are or where they came from. Don't worry. You are not supposed to go into the details of this.

This is, first and foremost, a book that will help you transition to a plant-based diet. You need a simple overview, not a lexicon of foreign words. Also, soon you will be introduced to many vegetarian products that will become your new favourites, and then you can safely choose these without scrutinising the ingredients lists all the time.

Fortunately for beginners, finding vegan food has never been easier, as store shelves are filling up with new vegan products, making it easy to find meat-, fish- and dairy-free alternatives. There are so many vegan manufacturers, and for now you just need to familiarise yourself with the selection and brand names of the different products, regardless of their specific content. Soon you will recognise them in the supermarket.

Of course, this first stage is both interesting and a bit challenging. You are navigating unfamiliar waters. You no longer include eggs, milk, cheese, fish, shellfish and meat in your diet. You read up on ingredients and you buy brand-new and hitherto unknown plant-based foods. Soon you find that you are warming to your new project, and that you are eagerly announcing your discoveries to family, friends and colleagues.

This introductory phase turns you into a conscious consumer by enhancing your knowledge of food ingredients and also making you rethink your eating habits, meal plans and food preferences. You will have a much larger repertoire of foods to shop for, you will cook new dishes, and soon you will be left with a more varied and hopefully veggie-rich diet.

By hopefully, I mean that you don't want to simply swap animal foods with processed plant-based substitutes. In the beginning, excluding dairy products, eggs and meat will get you far. Soon you will find that a lot of the plant-based convenience foods contain artificial ingredients – more soy protein than vegetables, for example. You want to reduce the use of these products as your vegan journey takes off and you will see that you really don't need to rely on them. More on this in week two of your meatless month.

nb!

Vegan and vegetarian food products are not the same. Ready-made products labelled 'vegetarian' often contain egg white, egg protein, powdered milk, etc. Throughout your 28 plant-based days, you want to take a look at the ingredients lists to make sure you are choosing foods that do not contain any animal ingredients.

today's task

Go to the largest and most well-stocked supermarket near you. Ask for 'allergy free' food products and vegan products, and the staff will guide you to the right shelves. If asking for help is not for you (you know who you are, people!), then explore the shelves by yourself. Pick out two to three vegan products you've never tried before, and put them into your basket to use during the week.

Suggestions for shopping

Plant-based drinks. Try oat milk for sure, or choose from almond, rice, coconut or soy.

Plant-based yoghurt. Most supermarkets now have coconut yoghurt, oat yoghurt and soy yoghurt.

Beans, chickpeas and lentils pre-cooked in tins or packets. Choose organic varieties as often as you can.

Vegan cheese, cream and crème fraîche.

Tofu or preferably tempeh, which is fermented soya beans.

Vegan burgers made from, for example, beets, chickpeas or cauliflower.

Pumpkin seeds. Toast them in a frying pan for 1 minute. Sprinkle on salads, porridge and oven-roasted vegetables.

Chia seeds. Often used as a substitute for eggs, as well as in cakes and puddings.

Chia pudding

3 tbsp chia seeds
200ml almond or coconut milk
1 tbsp cocoa nibs or goji berries
a handful of blueberries or raspberries
½ tsp vanilla powder or stevia powder, to taste
1 tbsp coconut yoghurt, to serve

Mix all the ingredients except the coconut yoghurt in a bowl or jar. Stir or shake well. Cover and place in the fridge. Stir or shake again after 15 minutes. Do this in the evening and you have a ready-made breakfast the next day. Top it off with a dollop of coconut yoghurt.

You could always add the blueberries, raspberries or goji berries before serving instead of adding them into the mix initially. You choose.

breakfast

Serves 1

Overnight oats

80g porridge oats
1 tbsp chia seeds or flaxseeds
250ml plant-based milk or water
a sprinkle of ground cinnamon
coconut flakes, chopped nuts and
  raisins, to serve

Mix everything in a bowl or jar. Chill in the fridge overnight. In the morning, top with coconut flakes, chopped nuts and raisins.

With the help of this book, you will learn some simple ways to cook nourishing meals without following a recipe. So, it's about understanding how to combine simple ingredients and make them into a complete meal.

go all in

Be firm.

Smokers finally manage to quit smoking when they go all in 100 per cent, as opposed to allowing themselves to smoke occasionally. The same way works for changing what you eat; you will succeed in your 28 days as a vegan when you stay away from meat and dairy products completely. Sure, you may be tempted to eat a slice of pizza with ham and cheese. Stay away. Even a mouthful will tempt you to have more. Hold yourself accountable and commit to the fact that everything that is not vegan is a no go for 28 days. Focus on these coming four weeks only. Who knows what will happen after your meatless month is over? You will cross that bridge when you come to it. Make the change. Seize the day. Make an effort to go beyond what you thought you had in you.

Now is the time to take note of two things, two big bonus awards that you gain by becoming vegan: one is that you will soon notice you are more energised with an improvement in your wellbeing. You will feel healthier, lighter and leaner – both at heart and physically. Please be patient. There is more to come. You may notice that your digestion becomes more regular and smoother than before. You may notice that avoiding sugar and sweets and refined carbohydrates has a stabilising effect on your blood sugar. This in turn is essential to achieving a balanced mood and keeping your ideal weight.

And two: you are about to notice the transformation of your taste buds. Slowly but surely it becomes easier and more natural to opt out of unhealthy snacks and 'empty' carbohydrates in favour of healthier choices. During these 28 days, I guarantee you that you will eat foods you have never tried before, either by preparing vegetables in a new way with new herbs and spices, or by testing new vegan foods available at the supermarket. You will move towards wellness, both emotionally and physically. Remember to be aware that this is related to the way you eat now.

Often we tend to eat our food too fast without paying proper attention to the flavours and taste. Now that you've changed your diet, your open mind will be more alert to palate experiences, not least the different tastes of sweet, bitter and sour, as well as the smell. It is a natural effect of taking control of what you eat: you become more conscious of what you put in your mouth. Remember to chew your food well, and notice the taste and smell of everything you eat in the future!

You would probably not sign an important contract without reading the content first, would you? The same should go for allowing food into your body without knowing what it is. With this book in hand you will know what you need to eat to succeed – and stay healthy. You will learn the basics of putting together a nutritious meal. This is especially important if you have health concerns such as obesity, diabetes, high cholesterol or painful joints. The more you learn about putting together meals with the right amount of carbohydrates, proteins, fat and fibre, the greater the health benefits. You need a little bit of everything, and many find that they stay satisfied for much longer on a plant-based diet than on a traditional meat-rich diet.

Did I mention you're going to get leaner? While this is not a weight-loss diet, it is safe to say that if you want to lose weight, becoming vegan will help you out.

Keep eating hummus. Hummus is the best secret weapon a vegan has, and you can use it for just about anything. Eat a large spoonful of hummus if you get hungry before dinner, put hummus on lettuce, try it as a topping on a baked sweet potato, or as a vegetable dip.

ps.

Join the Greenstuff.no group on Facebook to see what the alumni from 'How to be vegan in 28 days' are eating! Also, follow @lailamadso on Instagram for even more inspiration.

today's task

What do you need to know to give a good answer to anyone curious about how to survive on a vegan diet? Well, you can start with the fact that the health authorities recognise a plant-based diet as a healthy way of eating! A properly designed vegan diet gives you enough vitamins and minerals, enough protein and lots of fibre – and it's low in saturated fat. This book teaches you how to build a balanced plate of protein, carbohydrates, fibre and fat. However, you might want to take a B12 and a vitamin D supplement if you choose to continue as a vegan beyond these 28 days (see Day 13 for more on supplements).

A plant-based plate is one-third protein – beans, lentils, peas, often some form of plant-based meat made from soy or pea-protein – one-third vegetables and one-third wholefood sources of carbohydrates, such as sweet potato, brown rice and whole grains, and 1 tablespoon of fat from nuts, seeds and olive oil.

Many beginners are concerned about getting too little protein. With plants being your only source of protein, make sure at least one of your meals each day consists of legumes such as lentils, chickpeas and beans, seeds like pumpkin, sesame and sunflower, grains like oats, nuts like cashew nuts and almonds, and an assortment of vegetables of all colours of the rainbow.

An additional task for those who are thinking about weight: weigh yourself and note it down in your diary.

eating out and at work

Cooking your own vegan food at home is one thing. But what do you do at a restaurant, at work or when travelling?

Ordering plant-based at a restaurant is becoming easier and easier. Many restaurants have vegetarian dishes on the menu, and chefs can be flexible and creative when faced with a vegan challenge.

Always check for vegetarian options if there is nothing vegan on the menu. Most vegetarian dishes can often be made vegan. Let the waiter know that you are vegan, and that you fancy a vegetarian dish on the menu. For example, 'I'm a vegan, so I don't eat milk,

eggs, fish sauce and butter. Will the chef be able to remove these when cooking this dish?' Please be patient. There are still some staff and waiters who don't know the difference between vegetarian and vegan. The goal is that after you are done with this book you should be able to go out for dinner and order a meal exactly the way you want it: filling, delicious and totally vegan — something that is not offered on the menu. It's all about know-how. Make it easier on yourself and go to a restaurant you already trust, or check the menu beforehand. One tip is to go to a Thai, Indian or Mexican restaurant, as these often serve a selection of plant-based dishes.

There are some clever tricks to expanding the menu to get your own customised vegan meal. All these tricks you can use when travelling and staying in hotels, too.

3 ways to have it your way if there are no vegan options on the menu:

1 Look for vegetarian dishes instead. Sometimes it is just the sauce, topping or dressing that prevents a vegetarian dish from being vegan. The waiter will explain which animal products the different vegetarian dishes have. Then you suggest which ingredients to replace them with. Usually there is no problem to replace butter with olive oil, and cheese or sour cream with a salsa or, if you are lucky, even a vegan pesto.
2 Call the restaurant in advance and explain. As long as you give them a little heads up, the chef may be happy to prepare a delicious custom-made vegan meal based on the ingredients they have available in the kitchen. Don't be surprised if the rest of your dinner party look longingly at your plate as the food arrives at the table . . .
3 Order extra starters or sides instead of a main. Eating many small plates as a tapas meal is a smart way to eat vegan. If you like, ask the kitchen to put all dishes on a large plate and serve together as a main course.

A typical problem many vegans have is that their office cafeteria only offers traditional meat dishes. The Meatless Mondays they offer once a week will only get you so far if the buffet is filled up with classics like beef tacos, chops, fish and chips, pasta carbonara, spaghetti Bolognese or club sandwiches the remaining days of the week. Let the staff at your work cafeteria know you are plant-based, to see if there is something they can do for you. And talk to the HR department and challenge them for a greener selection at the buffet.

Try this simple and filling vegan work lunch:

Place two wholegrain slices of bread on a plate. Pour over a tablespoon of olive oil or Dijon mustard dressing, or drizzle over a few drops of balsamic or soy sauce. Keep loading up with every vegetable you can see. Tomato slices, cucumber slices, lettuce leaves, sugar snap peas, olives, beans, artichokes and bell peppers are often available. Top it all with fresh basil leaves or other herbs. Finally trickle over a little olive oil and a sprinkle of salt and pepper.

This also works well when you are staying at a hotel. Don't be afraid to ask the hotel staff for vegan alternatives, extra virgin olive oil and fresh herbs.

let the staff know that you are vegan.

today's task

Go to a restaurant, either your favourite one or someplace you haven't been before, and make an effort to order a custom-made vegan meal not offered on the menu. Try the actions you've learned and talk to the staff.

nb!

We eat pasta a maximum of one or two times a week, and we almost exclusively use vegetable varieties. Bean pasta, red lentil pasta, chickpea pasta, buckwheat pasta, sweet potato pasta and algae pasta provide more protein, and contain less carbohydrates, than regular wholewheat pasta.

A spiraliser is a great kitchen tool for a healthier low-carb pasta. Use one to make spaghetti-like strips of vegetables and then pour the sauce over in the usual way. I like to eat the vegetable spirals raw, but you can put them in the frying pan for two minutes to get a rounder flavour before you pour the hot pasta sauce over. It's a new way to eat pasta!

Pasta is everyone's favourite, and spaghetti Bolognese is popular family food. Fortunately, it is super easy to turn this classic meat sauce into a plant-based version. As a vegan chef you have to find new solutions, and a little humour sets a good tone at the dinner table. In vegan circles, it is fun to rename classic meat dishes. Spaghetti Bolognese is called spaghetti veganese. The French meat stew boeuf bourguignon is called 'bluff bourguignon' and Parmesan is called 'parmvegan'. Now that you've started to take notice, you'll probably start seeing this type of vegan meme everywhere. Have a laugh and challenge your family members to give your vegan dishes a name!

Here is a new secret weapon that you can serve at short notice when your family wants pasta, or you get an unexpected dinner guest on a weekday. At my house we typically make this on Sundays and serve it with spaghetti – our favourite spaghetti veganese! We use protein-rich beans or lentils in the sauce to make it extra filling.

super-easy spaghetti veganese

1 tbsp olive oil
1 onion, finely chopped
1–2 garlic cloves, finely chopped
½ tsp chilli flakes (optional)
2 x 400g tins of chopped tomatoes, preferably sweet plum tomatoes
2 carrots, grated
1 or 2 handfuls of tarragon or basil leaves
sea salt and freshly ground black pepper
spaghetti, to serve

Heat the olive oil in a large frying pan over medium heat. Add the onion, garlic and chilli flakes, if using, and cook for 5 minutes until the onion has softened. Stir in the tomatoes, carrots and basil, and season with salt and pepper. Cook for 20 minutes until the tomatoes have broken down a little in the sauce. Eat immediately or cool and store in an airtight container in the fridge.

pro tip This tomato sauce is the perfect base for vegan lasagne! To make vegan béchamel sauce, which is also used in lasagne, simply follow the traditional recipe, but swap dairy butter for either margarine or a few tablespoons of olive oil. I prefer to use soya milk as a substitute for cow's milk, as I think nut milk alternatives are a little too sweet for white sauce. As always, I prefer gluten-free flour or spelt, and add salt and pepper to taste. This is all you need to make a creamy white vegan béchamel. Béchamel sauce is used in other pasta dishes, potato gratin, cauliflower cheese and moussaka, among other dishes.

stock up your kitchen with basics

Give a little love to your kitchen cabinets during your 28 days as a vegan. Be generous and a bit experimental when filling the shelves.

Stock them with sugar-free mueslis, whole grains like spelt and oats, legumes, such as red and green lentils, cannellini beans and black beans. Chickpeas and chickpea flour. Wild rice. Quinoa, the protein-rich seed that can be used in the same way as rice, is also available as flour. Nuts and seeds. Wholegrain pasta and different types of bean pasta. Make sure to always have a variety of these dry goods in your house. And don't forget vegetable broth! Start with just a few and carry on stocking up on plant-based foods little by little. Have a look at the list of dry goods on page 20.

You also need at least one jar of tahini, and maybe miso paste. (We'll return to miso later on.) By the way, did you know that tahini is full of B vitamins, which are important for vegans, and that miso is good for gut health? Tamari is the gluten-free variety of soy sauce, and many people prefer it due to its high quality. Red and green curry pastes are always nice to have. Tinned coconut milk adds wonderful taste and healthy fats. Raisins, dried apricots and dried cranberries are great in salads, or in porridge and desserts. Dates add sweetness to smoothies. Do buy jars of olives and capers, as well as Dijon mustard, apple cider vinegar, white wine vinegar, cold pressed extra virgin olive oil, coconut oil and different plant milks. Maybe you have some of these vegan essentials already, and if not you're about to invest in your future healthier eating habits.

Using fresh herbs and all kinds of spices makes all the difference in the art of cooking. Play around with them and notice how they elevate the taste of a meal from dull to exciting.

The goal is that eventually you don't need to go shopping every time you want to cook a meal. Of course, you are not going to buy everything I have listed here all at once. Just choose a few products. Little by little, your kitchen cabinet will be filled up with what you need.

And again, remember there is no need to study a bunch of new recipes in order to cook vegan dishes during these 28 days. The recipes in this book are the ones I consider to be my vegan kick-starters. But, more importantly, you will learn simple cooking principles. Peel, cut, steam, bake, cook, pan-fry, grate or eat raw. Carrots, sweet potatoes, beetroot, tomatoes, onions, garlic, kohlrabi, squash, avocado, sprouts, artichoke, olives, asparagus, celery, Jerusalem artichokes . . . the list goes on.

nutritional yeast!

This is a flavour enhancer that works wonders in vegan food. It is one of the few new things I really recommend that you buy sooner rather than later during your 28 days vegan. Nutritional yeast is not ordinary yeast and cannot be used to make bread rise. It gives food a cheesy, slightly nutty taste, a bit like Parmesan, and it is full of the wonderful umami flavour.

food prepping

Food prepping has become very trendy both on social media and in the real world over the past year. Doing your food prep for the week, for example on weekends when you have extra time, will be well-spent hours. Taking into account what you already have in your cupboards, write a shopping list for the upcoming week's dinners, or at least four of them, buy the ingredients and prepare those dinners. This means cutting up ingredients and cooking sauces and dressings for the week to come. It may sound boring, but life gets a lot easier and you have time to do fun things after work instead of spending your time cooking from scratch every day. Besides, it's wonderful not to have to think about what to have for dinner every single day. This way, you have already planned your dinner menu for the coming week. If that's not a weight off your shoulders, I don't know what is!

Store your sauces in airtight glass containers in the fridge, or freeze in portions. Food stored in airtight containers can be left conveniently for two days in the fridge. But check that the temperature is not above 2–4°C. If you put food in the freezer, you can eat it at any time during the week.

Always save your leftovers — let your kids in on it and teach them the value of never throwing out food, or at least as little food as possible.

Today I suggest you plan something that is easy to prepare. Roasted root vegetables pretty much take care of themselves in the oven while you do the rest of your food prep. Why don't you try the Salt-Baked Beets with Beetroot Hummus on page 140.

Serve the beets with a generous dollop of vegan mayonnaise on top. Vegan mayo tastes great on all vegetables, and is my absolute favourite after hummus. When making mayonnaise you get to use another fantastic vegan ingredient, aquafaba. This is the liquid from a tin of chickpeas and it can be used instead of egg whites as it whips up to the same texture when you beat it. See page 157 for how to make your own Vegan Mayonnaise.

today's task

Choose two or three dishes from this book, such as the beets suggested opposite, or anything else that you fancy. Write a shopping list of all the foods you need, and keep in mind that you want to cook a generous dinner in order to have leftovers for another meal.

Continue reading the lists of ingredients on food labels. Look for organic products and compare prices with non-organic products.

shortcuts and soaking

Since clearing your kitchen shelves and shopping for vegan ingredients, you've probably started experimenting with new dishes.

Now is the time to go a little deeper into how a freshly baked vegan fits into a busy everyday life. It is smart to learn both some cooking shortcuts and a few simple steps that make your shopping more efficient. Don't be surprised if you find that your food budget stretches further than before. Eating vegetables is not at all expensive, as long as you plan ahead.

That said, frozen food is quick and convenient. Frozen vegetables such as peas, wok vegetables, Brussels sprouts, spinach and broccoli will rescue you on those evenings you're home late from work and have little or no time to prepare dinner. Studies have shown that frozen vegetables retain much of their nutritional value, and they taste good steamed or stir-fried. Pour over a tablespoon of nice extra virgin olive oil and sprinkle over a pinch of sea salt.

By the way, while you're standing there head down at the freezer counter, do check out the chilled vegan goods. Pick up a pack of fishless fishcakes, vegetable pot pie or an oven-baked jackfruit pizza. Even though 28 days vegan is all about cooking wholefoods and vegetables, ready-made can be a life saver from time to time. I recommend you are conscious about consuming wheat flour and sugar, but you are not supposed to be ascetic; it is acceptable to indulge occasionally in junk food. Just don't do it five days a week.

beans and chickpeas can soak for 8-12 hours.

Make healthier choices when you can, like my favourite homemade pizza option: use sweet potato slices as a pizza crust instead of your standard dough. I'll remind you that the goal of this book is to inspire you to put together and prepare vegetables, and turn them into hearty nutritious meals without a recipe. My dinner suggestions are only meant as encouragement and a guide for home cooking.

Okay. Now we can continue our shopping trip — you have had your head in the freezer for too long!

Pick up tins of chopped tomatoes, chickpeas, beans and lentils. There are excellent organic brands in most supermarkets. Even better is going to a world food store or health food store and bulk buying dried beans and lentils. They are even more flavourful, not to mention cheaper, than tinned.

It will vary slightly, but a rough estimate is that the volume of beans, lentils and peas doubles after they are soaked and cooked.

How long beans and lentils need to soak depends, among other things, on size. Beans and chickpeas can often soak for 8–12 hours, ideally overnight. Lentils and peas usually take 2–3 hours. If you are pressed for time, you do not need to soak yellow, brown and red lentils for more than 10 minutes. Remember to rinse well before cooking. Nuts, seeds, rice and grains can also be soaked to increase nutrient uptake, as they contain phytic acid and enzyme inhibitors, which interfere with digestion. Soaking removes these enzyme inhibitors and thus means better absorption of nutrients. Anything you want to soak should be rinsed under cold running water first.

nb!
Talking about rice: you want to rinse and soak wild rice and brown rice before cooking, and preferably cook it in more water than indicated on the package. Why? To remove arsenic and phytic acid, which inhibit nutrient uptake in your gut.

Then, before cooking, rinse well again, and fill a large pot of cold water to cover it all. Let it simmer under a lid and remove any foam that builds up. The legumes are done when they are tender or even al dente, just like with pasta. Also remember that tinned lentils and beans will need shorter cooking times.

See the list of my favourite ingredients on page 16. Stock up on sweet potato, cauliflower, tomatoes, lemons, onions and celeriac. These kinds of vegetables stay fresh for a long time and are solid ingredients in a plant-based diet. Feel free to pick avocados, fresh spinach and lettuce as well. Buy a cabbage and I will soon teach you how to cook it! Make a casserole, or fresh cabbage in season is heavenly grilled or roasted.

Brown rice, wild rice and quinoa are always nice to have. Asians are among the longest-living people on Earth, and rice is one of their cooking staples. Drop white rice — at least while you follow this book. White rice provides little nutrition and spikes your blood sugar. Try wild rice or brown rice instead. Wild rice can be found in health food stores, and brown rice or wholegrain rice is easily found at the supermarket.

Pick up plant milks at the supermarket. Again, oat milk is preferable, and not just because it is sustainable. Many people find it easier to digest than soya milk. Rice milk tastes very sweet, but works well in porridge, smoothies, cakes and cocoa.

Start tonight: soak beans overnight and eat them tomorrow! How about soaking chickpeas and making Falafel with Pickled Onions tomorrow? See the recipe on page 134.

protein and performance

Now that you have filled your kitchen cabinets with useful plant-based ingredients, you have everything you need to cook some seriously good vegan stuff. As you gain more knowledge, you will gain more and more confidence cooking vegan meals from scratch.

A few days ago, I introduced the benefit of building a plate with the right amount of protein, carbohydrates, fat and fibre. One question you often encounter as a vegan is, 'How do you get protein if you don't eat meat?' The truth is that plant-based diets are in fact a good source of protein, the body's important building block. In fact, a number of the world's top athletes have switched to a plant-based diet to optimise their health. The list includes racing car drivers, football players and Olympic weightlifters. In interviews with these athletes, it appears that several of them quit meat to get rid of inflammation and stress in the body. British boxer David Haye has won several World Cups as a vegan. He cut out meat and dairy products after doing research on which diet could most effectively help him recover from a shoulder injury. Sprint legend Carl

Lewis with nine Olympic golds switched to the vegan diet late in his career. He now considers going vegan as instrumental to his greatest sports achievements. Tennis player Venus Williams made her comeback on the court after she changed to a plant-based diet when injuries were about to put an end to her career.

In 2017, the world's most famous racing car driver, Lewis Hamilton, won his fourth Formula 1 World Cup after he converted to a plant-based diet. Afterwards, he stated, 'In my 32 years, I've never felt better.' Not only have they been able to meet their high protein demands through a plant-based diet but they also cite a stronger cardiovascular system, better cholesterol levels, better sleep and better concentration to boot.

What you need to know is that our daily protein need is not as great as many claim, and the belief that protein is only found in meat is outright wrong. Protein should account for around 10–20 per cent of your total energy consumption during an average day. In comparison, as much as 25–40 per cent of total daily calories should come from fat. In fact, you need less protein and more fat in your diet than you might think.

Choosing wholefoods and vegetables consciously to build up a balanced mix of nutrients – including proteins – will keep you covered.

Steamed broccoli with a little olive oil is lovely for dinner, and many people know that broccoli is healthy and contains lots of fibre and vitamins. The fact that broccoli also provides plenty of protein is perhaps a surprise to many. Serve broccoli with hummus and you will get more than enough protein. It isn't necessary to have a piece of meat as well. If you also happened to start off your day with Overnight Oats (see page 30) for breakfast, you've got your daily protein needs covered. So worrying about protein deficits on a plant-based diet is unnecessary, yet it is smart to be aware of these things. If you supplement vegetable dishes with protein-rich nuts, seeds such as pumpkin seeds and legumes such as lentils, you are on the safe side.

Therefore, today, on Day 9, you will get to learn about protein-rich vegan foods, so that you, and everyone around you, can rest assured you are in the best possible care while you're doing 28 days vegan.

Protein satisfies and keeps you feeling full for longer.

Here's an overview of hearty foods that are good sources of protein:

Hummus. A chickpea-based dip originally from the Middle East. Common side dish at most plant-based restaurants, and your local supermarket will sell it too. Soon, however, you will never buy ready-made hummus again. It is super easy to make your own. See page 151.

Tofu. Available in different varieties, but most popular in cooking is the one that comes as a firm solid block. Tofu is made from soya beans and has a high nutritional content and low fat content. Cook it with spices, herbs or soy sauce, or marinate it in chilli oil for an hour, or whatever flavouring you fancy. Crumbled and stir-fried tofu is a great substitute for scrambled eggs, and tofu cut into cubes is perfect in Asian curry sauces based on coconut milk. Be aware that tofu can be hard to digest, so limit your use. Remember what I said about soy products on Day 2.

Tempeh. Made from fermented soya beans. Tempeh is a bit like tofu, but with a nutty flavour. Loaded with umami, which gives tempeh a pungent taste. The fermentation process makes it more digestible than tofu.

Quinoa. High in protein. Use in the same way as rice.

Peas. Frozen or fresh. You can also buy pea protein at the health-food store to add to smoothies or vegetable juices.

you need less protein and more fat in your diet than you might believe.

Edamame beans. Similar to peas, but larger and fleshier.

Beans and lentils. Choose between kidney beans, cannellini, pinto, black, lima beans and chickpeas (chickpeas are sometimes called garbanzo beans in cookbooks).

Seeds. Sunflower seeds, pumpkin seeds, sesame seeds, chia seeds, flaxseeds. Crush them in a mortar to make available even more nutrition that is hidden behind the shell. Use them in salads, for baking bread, mix them into a serving of quinoa and sprinkle them on all kinds of food.

Nuts and nut butter. A vegan's Dream Order! You've probably tasted peanut butter, but what about almond butter, cashew butter or walnut butter? Eat a handful (not much more) of mixed nuts to satisfy your hunger and get control over your blood sugar. Don't forget pecans, brazil nuts, pistachios and pine nuts.

All of these protein sources are excellent basic foods to have to hand. They contain a healthier type of fat than animal foods, plus slow-release carbohydrates to keep blood sugar stable and fibre for optimal digestion – not to mention vital vitamins and minerals.

today's task

Make a meal based on tofu or tempeh, such as the Broccoli and Tofu on page 118. If you are using firm tofu, first squeeze out the water by placing the whole block on a platter, or cut it into 1cm-thick slices, cover with paper towels, place a heavy dish or bowl on top and leave it for 10 minutes or so. This way the tofu absorbs even more of the flavour from spices or marinades. (As mentioned, this only applies to firm tofu. Silken tofu is soft and should not be pressed.)

Pan-fry it in slices or large cubes over a medium heat with a little oil and a sprinkle of salt. The tofu is ready when golden. Pour soy sauce over and cook for a few minutes until slightly crispy. Serve with steamed broccoli, sprinkled with salt and drizzled with a little olive oil.

Don't fancy tofu? Make a dish based on quinoa such as the Roasted Butternut Squash with Quinoa on page 104. Quinoa is as easy to cook as rice – simply follow the directions on the packet. Quinoa can be served in a simple way too; try it with hummus and lightly cooked carrots, and drizzle over extra virgin olive oil and a sprinkle of sea salt.

satiety and blood sugar

We have already declared hummus to be a vegan's best friend. Adding dressings and other sides is a wonderfully easy way to turn any regular vegetable dish into a hearty green and nutritious delicacy. Pickled red onions, cashew cream, peanut sauce, artichoke dip, tahini dressing, beetroot hummus and last but not least good old guacamole are examples of wholesome sides that not only enhance the taste but also the satisfying feeling you want after a meal. Smart superfoods for vegans!

No one needs to leave the table hungry after a plant-based dinner. On the contrary. You will soon find that you will always be perfectly nourished provided you have a properly balanced plant-based diet. Plants and vegetables satisfy you in part because they are full of fibre that fills your stomach without adding a lot of calories — unlike meat and dairy products that do not provide any fibre at all, only a lot of fat. This means many vegans find that they can allow themselves

slightly larger portions — and still keep their ideal weight. Adding to that, fibre rich veggies are good for stabilising your weight because fibre helps keep your blood sugar from spiking and crashing. Balanced blood sugar takes away your desire for sweets and snacks and you feel fuller for longer. The total effect is simple: a vegan diet helps to maintain your ideal weight.

However, keep in mind that the typical vegan condiments may be made from high-fat foods such as nuts, oils and seeds. Seeds and nuts should be eaten in moderation. Cashew cream, peanut sauce and nutty toppings are meant to accessorise your meal — not cover it. One or two tablespoons should be enough.

Vegan dishes taste even better when you manage to assemble different food textures. Try toasting pumpkin seeds or capers in a pan with a little oil and a pinch of salt to create a wonderful crunchy texture when sprinkled on top of veggies.

today's task

Make two dips or dressings from the recipe section in this book. Pour them into airtight glass jars or whatever airtight containers you have. Store them in the fridge and use for your meals over the coming days. Hummus is the No 1 vegan rescue for most meals, and if you haven't made hummus yet, it's time. Chickpeas give you minerals for your bones and B vitamins for a strong psyche and healthy mind. In this book you will get a recipe for four different varieties of hummus.

I like a deeper flavour to my hummus that I create by adding caramelised onions and garlic. See the recipe on page 151.

Your new secret weapon is pickled red onions and pickled red cabbage. You can preserve them separately, or why don't you make a mixture of the two. It's easy to make and enhances the flavour of absolutely anything you eat. I recommend it as a topping on veggie burgers or sandwiches, or as a sidekick to the Friday taco. You can find the recipe for Pickled Red Onions on page 155.

keeping delicacies such as hummus, vegan mayonnaise and pickled red onions and cabbage in your fridge gives you the upper hand anytime you need to prepare a quick-fix meal.

feeling good!

Do you remember that I said the first ten days as a vegan are the most challenging part of your 28-day journey? Congratulations! You've just proceeded one step further.

Now you're on your eleventh day without meat. Be conscious and notice how you feel. How are you doing? Note down a few keywords in the diary in the back of this book (see page 162). A feeling of lightness? Full of energy? Healthy digestion? Energy to exercise after work? Are you sleeping better and is it easier to get up in the morning? Begin to notice all the physical and mental changes you are going through, and be aware of these every day. Changing your diet may cause you to feel some temporary discomfort, like headaches or body aches, or maybe you find yourself a little bloated. This is completely normal. It just means that your body hasn't adjusted to your diet yet. Even more reason to take note of what you eat every day and connect the dots to your daily

mental and physical state. Bear in mind it can take about 14 days before the body begins to adapt, and then the positive aspects of a plant-based diet will become more evident every day. If you went all in and followed the plan, it's likely that you have noticed your sweet tooth has subsided and you have stopped snacking between lunch and dinner.

Many people who switch to a plant-based diet report they do it primarily for health reasons. In fact, vegans often report on diminishing or disappearing health problems. One of the most common positive changes people describe is that their skin becomes clearer and free of eczema and acne. Others find that their digestion improves, sinusitis disappears, hair and nails get stronger, and almost everyone will report a huge energy boost. Suddenly you realise you have an energy surplus, and instead of lying on the couch after dinner, you feel the urge to move. The fact that your sleep has improved will, of course, contribute to even more health benefits. Not only putting a smile on your face, but your family's too.

One sweet domino effect of better sleep is that feeling more rested with more energy can lead to more quality time and intimacy with your partner. Which in turn may awaken your — and your partner's — libido. Who knew being vegan could deliver an outcome like that!

It doesn't end there. Women thriving on a vegan diet may experience less menstrual cramps, and reduced symptoms of both PMS and menopause have been reported. In Asia, far fewer women suffer from menopausal symptoms, which can be attributed to the larger quantities of vegetables and soy products in their diet compared to the Western diet. Our digestive system is a complex one, and feeling this many positive side effects after changing your eating habits means that there is not necessarily one single cause why you feel better. Scientifically proven or not, it's worth trying a nutrient-dense plant-based diet if you have ailments like the ones we've mentioned above.

Beans and raw vegetables are often blamed for bloating, gassiness and intestinal problems, but there are many factors that come into play. If you experience symptoms such as bloating during your four plant-based weeks, try filling your plate with more protein-rich foods like oats, quinoa, wild rice and tofu or tempeh. Cut down on onions, garlic and ready-made soy products at the same time, and you may be better off. Continue to consciously adjust your diet over the 28 days and notice all improvements as they come along.

A major undefined health problem is inflammation, which often appears as stiffness and arthritis – the typical pain in the hips, knees and back that many of us wake up to every day. Eventually we get so used to it we accept the aches and normalise them. Often it is only when we get better or get rid of these joint ailments that we realise how bad it was. If you are one of those people living with soreness and pain, you should really thank yourself as you embark on your meatless month. Chances are you'll soon be better off. A plant-based diet free of processed food will have an anti-inflammatory effect on the body. Be aware that some vegetables are more beneficial than others when it comes to curbing inflammation. An anti-inflammatory diet should be low in starchy vegetables because they have a high glycaemic effect in the body, which can lead to inflammation. If you suffer from inflammation-induced ailments, you may want to cut down on corn, potatoes (sweet potatoes in moderation is okay) and parsnips. Note down the effect this has on your mental and physical state in the back of the book.

Golden milk

Golden milk is a delicious caffeine-free substitute for tea or for coffee latte in the afternoon. Drink it whenever you fancy something healthy instead of dessert or an evening snack.

250ml coconut milk or oat milk
½ tsp ground turmeric, or 4cm piece of
  fresh turmeric
½ tsp vanilla powder
a pinch of Ceylon cinnamon
a few drops of agave syrup
a small pinch of freshly ground
  black pepper

How to do it: if you're using fresh turmeric, scrape off the peel with the tip of a teaspoon. Finely grate it. Mix all the ingredients in a saucepan. Heat until just before boiling point and remove. Finished!

turmeric

is a common ingredient in India, as well as in Okinawa, Japan, which is one of the places in the world where the inhabitants have the highest longevity scores.
The yellow spicy turmeric root has been recognised in many research studies for its healing and anti-inflammatory properties. Turmeric is indeed a potent antioxidant, which means it neutralises free radicals. Thus, it's an anti-inflammatory, and there are studies indicating a positive correlation between taking turmeric and reducing the risk of cardiovascular disease. If you mix pepper with turmeric, you increase its nutrient absorption. Fat works as an important vehicle for nutrient absorption, so using a plant milk like oat or preferably coconut works well for your Golden milk (see page 53).

Be conscious of the connection between what you eat and how you feel during this phase.

Draw up two columns in your diary, with what you eat in one column and how you feel and any other comments in the other. Physical feelings, energy levels, melancholy, happy, full of pep, irritable, refreshed, excited, exercising, cycled to work, smiled to strangers on the bus, home cooking, happy family situation, surprised colleagues with your lunch choices, etc. The sole purpose of this is to start to see the connection between what you eat and how you feel. Replace unqualified opinions about what you *think* is the reason why you've slept poorly or are tired after dinner with more conscious *logical* conclusions related to what you have been eating for the past 24 hours.

wheat and convenience food

Now you're broken in and starting to feel quite confident. You've experimented with cooking vegetables, and you have even tried frozen fast food. We have talked about the importance of a nutritious and balanced diet.

Part of the plant-based plan in this book is crowding out wheat flour, white sugar, white rice and potatoes to make room for more nutrient-dense foods and grains. Try spelt, millet and farro, spelt sourdough bread, wild rice, sweet potato and, of course, lots of vegetables baked in the oven or stir-fried in a pan, steamed, raw or cooked. Opt out of 'empty' (nutrient-poor) white carbohydrates and go for foods that have a lower glycaemic profile and more nutrition — meaning, look for less starchy foods. Load up on vegetables and legumes, which are fibre-rich as well as carbohydrate-rich.

Next to sugar (which has many different names), wheat is a usual suspect in all kinds of convenience foods, and it is tricky to avoid. For example, it is hard to find a bread that doesn't have wheat flour among the first three

ingredients listed. However, keep looking for 100 per cent spelt bread, because it is much better for your health (and weight in the long run). Now that you're on the lookout for wheat flour, you will find it in a whole range of foods. At this stage, it is mostly about being aware of how often wheat is listed as an ingredient in the food you eat, as this will give you a good indication of how much it adds up weekly. The challenge is to switch to foods with no wheat, or at least less of it. Cooking at home will surely reduce your wheat consumption. Just know that you are doing yourself and everyone you cook for a great favour!

What does wheat flour have to do with a vegan month?

More and more health experts are unifying in the belief that avoiding wheat and gluten is good for us. After three to four weeks without sugar and gluten, many experience a marked improvement in energy levels, they sleep better at night, and generally have an improvement in their wellbeing, with a clear mind and good mood.

Cutting down on gluten can be quite tricky as a lot of convenience foods contain wheat. The same goes for all the unnecessary sugar we consume when we indulge in processed foods. In this book, you are encouraged to prepare simple homemade meals and gradually crowd out quick-fix ready-made foods. Consider this your golden ticket, and test a couple of weeks without wheat flour while you're at it! If you find that dropping sugar and wheat becomes too much, focus on being meat-free. You will, however, naturally become more aware of your intake of wheat and sugar during your 28-day journey.

Wheat and sugar are the underlying cause of many inflammatory disorders, not least any sore joints you may have. Reducing your intake of refined carbohydrates will improve your digestion. Perhaps the most evident outcome of all is that your craving for sweets subsides when you are not feeding your body with cookies and pastries. This in turn will of course make it easier for you to maintain your ideal weight.

Hooray for all the health benefits you are about to achieve — in addition to just detoxing from meat and dairy — and still you are only on the twelfth day. Make notes in your diary so that you hold yourself accountable and become more conscious of the link between what you eat and how you feel.

Make yourself familiar with gluten-free wheat alternatives:
Millet, rice flour, chickpea flour, almond flour, oats, coconut flour, quinoa flour, buckwheat, tapioca and teff flour.

tips

Make buckwheat bread or spelt bread (although spelt contains gluten it's a favourite among many people when they transition from regular wheat), try pancakes with lentils, beans and buckwheat flour, or my favourite, cauliflower patties.

ps.

Again, remember to limit your consumption of bread, pancakes and waffles if you want to lose weight. Such foods often contain refined grains and fast-release carbohydrates that are quickly converted into sugars in the body, increasing your blood sugar quickly and making it more difficult to lose weight.

Vegetarian ready meals

One of the fastest growing food categories is plant-based ready meals. Vegan spreads, vegetarian burgers, veggie minced meat, veggie hot dogs and other meat substitutes can save you on busy days, and will work fine if you're the only vegan at a family barbecue. Vegetarian and vegan products are often similar to animal meat both in looks and taste, and although many vegans don't want their food to look like an animal product, it may be convincing for your family. These substitutes work as a quick fix and make people see that it is possible to eat more meat-free foods. I am cheering for that!

The goal of this book is to help you eat more vegetables. Processed plant-based meat substitutes often contain very little wholefoods and are mostly based on soy protein, corn flour and salt (look for sodium in the ingredients lists). In addition, ready-made foods often contain wheat flour and a lot of sugar. My focus is on changing your eating habits to eating more vegetables, and teaching you basic cooking methods for plant-based foods. I believe you will enjoy the greatest effects if you plan a diet consisting mostly of wholefoods. That is why I inspire you to replace meat and ready-made foods with veggies as often as possible.

Take the Friday taco, for example. Soft wheat wraps or yellow corn tortillas, which are admittedly vegan, can easily be replaced with lettuce wraps. It is smart to crowd out your favourite processed foods if they contain refined carbohydrates. It's just a change of habit! Check out my recipe for Tacos with Five-Spice Fried Sweet Potato on page 128.

today's task

Today and throughout the rest of your meatless month, you want to crowd out as much wheat as possible with wheat-free alternatives such as millet, buckwheat, chickpea flour or quinoa flour. Even if spelt is related to wheat, spelt is a healthier option due to its higher content of protein and iron as well as other minerals. Also, become acquainted with the gluten-free products available at the supermarket. Replace white rice with brown rice and do try wild rice, which is a special type of grain, higher in protein than regular rice. Replace regular potatoes with sweet potatoes. Pasta with bean-based pasta. And remember, stay away from excessive sugar. To get rid of your liking for sweet-tasting foods, you need to stop feeding your sweet tooth. Keep checking the ingredients lists, and don't buy anything that has sugar in it. Your body will thank you with better sleep, better digestion, a better mood and thus better self-esteem! And possibly fewer joint ailments and pain in your knees, shoulders and hips.

health check and supplements

Eating primarily plant-based wholefoods will nourish your body and optimise the absorption of the essential vitamins and minerals it needs.

However, there are some important exceptions. We have talked about vitamin B12 already, and how it is found naturally in meat and dairy products. Every vegan should take a vitamin B12 supplement. Some vegan ready meals, plant milks and vegetable juices have added B12. In any case, I recommend that you take supplements as part of your daily morning routine. You can take B12 in addition to a vitamin B complex that contains several other types of B vitamins. Actually, research suggests that even people who do eat meat and dairy may very well be short on B12, so my advice is it's helpful for everyone to book a doctor's appointment to check your B12. You can take B12 either as tablets or sprays and you can also get B12 shots.

Another important vitamin is vitamin D which, with a few exceptions, is only found in animal foods. The natural way of getting your vitamin D is through the sun. However, Northern Europeans get so little sunshine in the dark winter months that we would all benefit from vitamin D supplementation from October to March.

When it comes to minerals, vegans can benefit by supplementing their diet with iodine and iron. Iodine deficiency is a common cause of hypothyroidism. Iodine is often added to regular table salt, or try downing a small glass of water each morning with a pinch of crushed bladderwrack or sea moss. There are also seaweed flakes that can be added to soups and smoothies. Iodine is also available as a kelp supplement.

In countries with typical Western diets, grains and other plant-based foods are an important source of iron. However, grains have anti-nutrients that can inhibit iron absorption. Soaking, sprouting and baking with sourdough will make the iron in plant-based foods more available for absorption. Brown bread, grains, chickpeas, peas, beans, lentils, vegetables, dried fruits such as figs and apricots all contribute a good deal of iron. Iron is better absorbed in the body when eaten with vegetables and fruits. This is because vegetables and fruits contain vitamin C and fruit acids, which increase the absorption of iron and also zinc. So make sure you drink a little orange juice with that slice of brown bread or your morning oats to ensure your iron absorption.

Conversely, you should avoid combining your veggie meals with coffee, tea or calcium-containing foods and beverages because calcium and tannic acid from tea and coffee inhibits iron uptake into the body.

As you can see, it is just as important for a vegan to get all the necessary vitamins and minerals as it is for everyone else. Many vegans, though, are aware of the need to eat a balanced diet and in fact, studies show that more than half of those who switch to a plant-based diet make their health a priority.

Vegans should also make sure they get enough calcium and choline, which non-vegans can get from dairy and eggs. Vegans who eat a balanced diet including lots of broccoli, cabbage, oats and whole grains should be covered.

today's task

Let this book be a reminder to take your health seriously. Book in with your GP today to check your level of B12, vitamin D and thyroid hormone. They are all blood tests. Ask your doctor to check your blood pressure as well. The reason you want to check your thyroid function is that it's connected to iodine deficiency as mentioned on the opposite page.

Remember to eat iron-rich foods at the same time as vitamin C-rich foods or drinks for increased iron absorption. If you single out breakfast for this purpose, it's easier to remember and keep track of.

Examples of iron-rich foods: lentils, chickpeas, tempeh, leaf cabbage, oats and quinoa.

new cooking skills

My motto: eat more vegetables! And best of all, you don't need many recipes to cook with vegetables! How?

This is all about looking at vegetables as delicious and satisfying foods. What it's not all about is a token salad of lettuce leaves, bell peppers, corn and sliced cucumber, which are nothing but a sorry excuse for vegan food. It is a classic beginner's mistake to fill up your plate with lettuce and raw veggies. This book teaches you how to cook with vegetables as the main ingredient of a meal. However, it should always be hearty, satisfying, tasty and tempting. Sweet potatoes, cauliflower, broccoli, beetroot, celeriac, beans, lentils and chickpeas complement each other; they can be mixed together as well as substituted for each other.

Now, choose a few vegetables to combine for dinner, and use the dishes later in this book as inspiration. Here is an example:

Sweet potatoes with chanterelles in herbal oil

Peel a sweet potato and cut it into wedges. Bring a large pan of water to the boil, and cook the wedges for 15 minutes. Meanwhile, dry-fry chanterelles in a pan to get rid of excess moisture. Then pour oil into the pan along with some garlic cloves and some finely cut spring onions, then fry further along with the sweet potato wedges. Serve the sweet potatoes and chanterelles by themselves, or spoon over a mixture of quinoa and fresh parsley. The oil from the chanterelles and sweet potatoes will soak into the quinoa mixture. Absolutely delicious. And filling and beautiful to look at. Your new culinary skills open up flexible solutions. If you do not have chanterelles, you know you can use Portobello mushrooms. And you can always substitute pumpkin or squash for sweet potato.

You could cook an even simpler dish than the one described above. Place the sweet potato wedges on a baking tray and bake them in the oven at 200°C/180°C fan/gas mark 6 for 30 minutes. Take the tray out of the oven and dollop on a spoonful of Vegan Mayonnaise (see page 157) or drizzle Sriracha Dressing (see page 157) all over the potato wedges. Toast some chopped almonds and sprinkle over the wedges. Serve with a green kale salad. It tastes lovely, and is 'just' vegetables without a name or recipe. You can cook any root vegetables in this way.

Have you tried salt-baked sweet potato yet? See my recipe on page 126 for inspiration. Or try the Roasted Butternut Squash with Quinoa, Kale and Crispy Pumpkin Seeds on page 104.

Obviously, I want you to replace meat with real vegetables. There are, however, lots of products made from vegetable protein to explore. Head over to the freezer counter, and you will find vegan mince that looks exactly like the minced meat you are used to. With your favourite spice it also achieves quite the same taste. Plant-based meat has to be seasoned just like actual meat. The same goes for tofu which many people use to replace meat.

What about dairy products? Here are some great tricks to help you reduce your use of dairy:

Butter can be replaced with coconut oil or olive oil in cooking, and there are many different types of plant butter for sandwich spreads – try coconut or rapeseed butter.

Milk is easy to replace with different types of plant milk. The most common alternatives are made from oats, almonds, soy, coconut or rice. There is even hemp milk and quinoa milk.

Cream can be replaced with coconut cream, soya milk with olive oil and silken tofu. Try whipping coconut cream for recipes that call for whipping cream.

Yoghurt made from oats and coconut are popular – try either natural or with berry and fruit flavours.

Cheese could very well deserve a chapter on its own. Many people find it very difficult to give up cheese. Actually, they say cheese is the main reason why vegetarians never switch 100 per cent to vegan. People have a passionate relationship with cheese, no doubt! That said, there are nice cheese substitutes to be had. You can buy many varieties of plant cheese that mimic mozzarella, Cheddar, feta or Jarlsberg, and they come in slices or blocks, or even grated for pizzas and tacos.

ps.

Find your favourite among the delicious vegan ice creams. Mine is peanut butter ice cream made with almond milk.

omega 3 and algae

It's essential for a vegan diet to be properly put together so that it contains all the nutrients you need for good health. Vegans are just as susceptible to eating far too much sugar and junk food as the next person. Luckily for you, there is little danger that, if you follow the plan in this book, you will end up being in a worse position than you were as an omnivore. A plant-based diet can also reduce the risk of lifestyle diseases, so you may even end up in a better position.

You are now learning the importance of a balanced diet while cutting out unnecessary sugar and refined carbohydrates. We've been talking about vitamins. You have learned that with the exception of vitamin B12, plant foods will provide all the nutrients you need.

Now it's time to talk about superfoods and algae. If you are a year-round veggie, you should, in addition to ensuring you get enough vitamin D, B12, iodine and iron, as we discussed in Day 13, also make sure you get enough omega 3. I am particularly concerned about omega 3 because our brain needs plenty of this essential fatty acid.

Thirty per cent of our brain consists of omega-3 fatty acids. Long-chain omega-3 fatty acids EPA and DHA are abundantly found in algae, wild fish and fish oils from Arctic regions. We have grown up with the belief that we should eat fish because it is healthy. As mentioned earlier, the omega-3 content of salmon and other fish is not as high as it was even a generation ago. New studies suggest that the omega-3 levels in the fish people eat today has dropped severely, which means you need to eat huge amounts of farmed salmon (which is the type of fish that most people eat) to get anywhere near enough. So salmon dinners are no longer a health guarantee. All the more reason to learn how to thrive on a nutritious plant-based diet. Omega 3 is also found in some plant oils, such as flaxseed oil, hemp oil and rapeseed oil, as well as in crushed flaxseeds, chia seeds and walnuts. However, the omega 3 from plants only contributes to ALA, which is a short-chain omega-3 fatty acid. Unfortunately there aren't as many documented health benefits of ALA as there are of the omega 3 from fish and algae.

The demand for fish oil has long been greater than the supply. International research is now underway to genetically manipulate rapeseed oil to contain potent levels of omega 3. Plant-based omega-3 oils from farmed algae that contain high amounts of EPA and DHA and that are free from pollutants have also been developed. It's your choice, but I do recommend that you take a potent omega-3 supplement, either a quality fish oil or an algae oil containing EPA and DHA during your 28 days — and beyond. Another fatty acid to consider is omega 6, which is found in high amounts in walnuts, safflower oil, sunflower seeds, hemp seeds and peanut butter. These are all good for the heart and body in moderate amounts; however, omega 6 can be pro-inflammatory, while omega 3 is important for its anti-inflammatory effects. The modern Western diet contains far more omega-6 fatty acids than necessary. In short, for good health you want to reduce your omega 6 and increase your omega 3.

Speaking of the richness of the sea: seaweed, especially purple nori, can provide vitamin B12. Furthermore, chlorella, a type of green algae that you can take in pill or powder form, also provides B12, as does the umami-rich seaweed dulce, popularly named 'the bacon of the sea'. Other types of algae, such as the superfood spirulina, contain B12; however the bioavailability in humans is poor.

Most algae are also rich in iodine and iron, which vegans should make sure they get enough of. Try kelp, which can be taken as a shot or poured into a smoothie. Previously I mentioned that the main source of iodine internationally is iodine-enriched table salt, and I recommend iodised Jozo salt.

flavour, fermenting and umami craving

Notice how many new vegetables and greens you have started eating since you embarked on your vegan journey.

In the past few weeks you have cooked plant-based food and experimented with new dressings and side dishes that you haven't even thought of before. Have you noticed that your sugar cravings have decreased, your mind feels clearer, and your body is charged with more energy than before? Take note of all changes. Understanding your own health and nurturing a conscious relationship with your mind and body will benefit you tremendously in the weeks to come. Again, keeping a food diary like the one in the back of this book connects the dots to how different food makes you feel, and it motivates you to develop good habits and make smart choices every day. Another extraordinary thing is that your taste buds mature. Start challenging yourself, and ask yourself: do I really need that sweet snack right now? Take advantage of the fact that your tongue has become more sensitive, and

avoid mindless eating. This also applies to fruity sugar-free chewing gums. Since going vegan, I've stopped chewing gum completely – both sweet and fresh flavours. I find it tastes chemically and awfully sweet. Now, I'm keener on foods with more advanced tastes.

It's time to take it one step further and introduce new flavours: welcome kimchi and kombucha.

Now that you eat less sugar and many more veggies – and soon fermented foods – you are strengthening your health – and gut – with every mouthful.

As you are removing old habits from your diet, it creates room to bring in healthier choices. Kimchi and kombucha are two exotic new substitutes for fruit salads, fruit juices and sweetened beverages. These probiotic superfoods are packed with fibre and lactic acid bacteria that may boost your gut, heart and brain. These two have the power to save you from over-eating sweets and cookies at those typical times when your energy is low. I'm not going to lie: it's an acquired taste, unfamiliar and maybe not what you were looking for. Up until now your taste buds have opted for sweet, or maybe salty snacks, or the popular combination of sweet and salty.

Instead, you hit the vegan jackpot and get the biggest bonus gift: UMAMI.

Sweet, sour, soft, full, smoked and hot – without being too strong. This is an attempt to describe the so-called fifth flavour, umami. Kimchi and kombucha are characteristically umami in taste. Miso too. Because the intake of fibre and probiotics strengthens your gut flora, the good bacteria developing in your gut send signals directly to the brain, which is picked up as a perfect craving for fermented foods. Previously, you experienced a sugar high after eating sweets and biscuits, now you will have – if you are lucky – a craving for kimchi or miso instead. If that happens, then you know that your gut flora is in top shape!

In recent years, intestinal health has become newsworthy and much talked about. At the same time, new research shows that there is a link between stress, anxiety, depression, dementia, autism and ADHD and an ever-increasing number of gastrointestinal disorders among the Western world. If you belong to the large group of people who are struggling, you may be glad that you have now taken steps towards a stronger gut flora.

today's task

Making kimchi and kombucha is quite feasible and can be an evening activity instead of baking bread. However, if starting up a fermentation experiment is a little too intimidating while following this 28-day plan, there are other ways to get your fermented fix. Fortunately, kimchi and kombucha can be found in health food stores and Asian supermarkets.

How much do you need? A glass of kombucha a day is a wonderful healthy habit, and two tablespoons of kimchi as a flavourful sidekick to your dinner a couple of times a week, is great for your gut health. Experiment a bit and see how you can incorporate kimchi into your diet.

Are you eager to start making something new? Why don't you try the Miso Dressing on page 159 and serve it with the Fried Rice with Edamame, Mushrooms and Carrots on page 142.

a glass of kombucha during the day is good for your gut health.

a new food culture + food waste

The world as we know it is changing.

The vegan population is increasing, and the demand for sustainable and non-toxic products is on the rise. Now the growing number of animal-borne illnesses, such as COVID-19, is accelerating the shift to a plant-based diet. Expert insights, as reported in the *Financial Times*, stated that US sales of meat substitutes had jumped a massive 200 per cent during the first eight-week period of the global pandemic in 2020.

The importance of health, nutrition and clean eating has extended its reach far beyond the health food establishments. Look no further than the bible of fine dining, the *Michelin Guide*, to see how the change is spilling out into every layer of society. Before, the finest restaurants were the ones that served classic French delicacies – based on meat and fish. Now, this seems old-fashioned and dated. The new kitchen is all about vegetables, and the Michelin stars are awarded to innovative chefs who largely use local produce and who leave as little environmental impact behind as possible. However, the real front-runners are the green-fluencers on social media who have not only inventive and experimental vegan profiles, but who want to shout out their green calling to the world. As the plant-based diet becomes more widely

recognised, today's plant eaters are gaining more confidence, and it is safe to say that the biggest culinary innovation is happening in the plant-based kitchen.

Nordic cuisine has been somewhat of a pioneer of this green kitchen trend. For one, pickled vegetables like red cabbage and kale are heavily rooted in Nordic food culture. Indeed, our home-grown traditions are not that different from vegetarian food culture in Asia. The sauerkraut is a Western variation of the Eastern speciality kimchi. The enzymes and the good bacteria that are formed by fermentation in food like this, does wonders for digestion and can help make beans and legumes easier to digest.

This month, you're in the driver's seat when it comes to turning away from a traditional meat- and dairy-rich diet towards a contemporary plant-based global food culture. You are now a source of inspiration for those around you, and not just your immediate family who enjoy your cooking on a daily basis. Colleagues and acquaintances on social media also learn about your vegan project – you suddenly choose differently to your old restaurant favourites and you can't help but share your new vegan experiences with anyone who cares to listen. It turns out that it's quite hard to shut up about such an important thing as a dietary change.

You will also see that becoming more conscious of what you eat affects you in several ways. By now, you have already experienced how what you eat affects your daily wellbeing, and that home-cooked food is cheaper and healthier than ready-made food wrapped in plastic. You have even noticed your taste buds changing, and you're craving fewer sweets than before.

The next step is to consider the amount of food you put on your dinner plate.

A standard serving of food is no longer what it was before. We fill up on portions twice as large as those of our grandparents, and not only that, we don't think twice about a second helping, even when we are more than satisfied by the first one.

Neither our health nor the environment benefits from this. Every Norwegian throws out on average over 42 kilos of food a year, and an average family in the UK wastes £700 worth of food every year, according to a study from the Waste and Resources Action Programme. Food waste is a huge global environmental problem, and the actions you take in your household will help to meet the UN target of halving global food waste by 2030. The easiest thing you can do is to put a little less food on your plate. The other thing you can do, of course, is to take care of any leftovers and store them in the fridge for the next day. That way, you also save on time. Feel free to read Day 7 again for a refresher on food prep.

today's task

It is really dreary to spend money on lots of delicious fruits and vegetables just to find that you are not able to eat them before they spoil. A number of green-fluencers have emerged on social media who inspire us to reduce food waste. Search online for inspiration and hold yourself accountable.

3 ways to reduce food waste:

1 Fill a bowl with cold water and add withered veggies like tomatoes, root vegetables, cucumbers, lettuce leaves and sugar snap peas. Put the bowl in the fridge or fill it with ice cubes as the water gets lukewarm. After 3–4 hours the vegetables will have become fresh and crispy again. Also remember that brown bananas and soft apples and carrots are great for smoothies.

2 When serving dinner, whether it is every day or at the weekend, be conscious of how much food each person actually needs. Do not serve larger portions than necessary. Cooking too much food (without taking care of leftovers) and putting too much food on everyone's plate is outright food waste and throwing money right out the window. Needless to say, putting large servings on everyone's plates could ruin both your weight plan and health.

3 Check what vegetables and fruits you have left before you go to the shops. Then adjust your shopping list so that you do not buy more of the same, and use up what you have before you buy more of the same produce.

Beyond Meat burger, anyone?

As the world is becoming increasingly aware of issues regarding health, climate and animal welfare, sales of vegetarian food products are increasing. There are now a wide variety of vegan spreads and meat alternatives that taste close to what you are used to. In fact, I believe that when you try these vegan products for the first time, it is likely you will enjoy them so much they will become your new normal, even after your 28 days are over. That said, your sandwich will look just as good filled with wholefoods like avocado, nut butter, coconut butter, olive tapenade, hummus, beetroot, cucumber and tomato slices with a pinch of sea salt and a drizzle of olive oil.

In a transitional phase and in emergencies, it is more than okay to look for plant-based meat replacements, such as vegan burgers and sausages. However, if you eat these ready-made solutions at the expense of your five veggies a day, you will add too much sugar and fat to your diet.

Any convenience foods, as well as meat substitutes, are high in calories and will likely contain more salt and sugar than the piece of meat they replaced. In addition, ready-made veggie products often contain hard-to-digest soy protein, as well as sunflower oil, which you don't want to eat too often. Also, be aware that vegetarian products are usually based on egg protein and therefore are not vegan. You risk both putting on weight and upsetting your stomach if you eat a lot of meat substitutes like this.

However, no matter what one thinks of ready meals and meat substitutes, they are the key to getting more people to opt out of meat and to move on to a plant-based diet. I salute that! At the same time, I encourage you to learn from this book and choose wholefoods and vegetables whenever you can.

Take, for example, the Impossible Burger, the vegan patty that has somehow become a kind of veggie-burger rock star. When it launched, there were high expectations. Vegan foodies went crazy and were (mostly) over the moon all over social media. Admittedly, this burger looks impressive, with the same thickness as the meat it's replacing. Some people like it, others say it tastes rather unconvincing. The content may still be the most surprising thing about it. It is made from soy protein concentrate, sunflower oil, potato protein, soy protein isolate, salt and water, and is glued together with modified food starches, methylcellulose and many more ingredients that are difficult to pronounce.

Likewise, the Beyond Meat burger has taken the food industry by storm. The Beyond Burger mimics the taste, look and feel of real beef, and it has become very popular, not only among vegans, but also with hungry carnivores and fast-food lovers. Just like the Impossible Burger, the Beyond Burger is made using chemical additives and highly processed plant protein. Instead of soy, the Beyond Burger is made from pea protein, which may be more digestible than soy, but otherwise the ingredients lists of the two burgers aren't really that different. They both contain omega-6-rich vegetable oils, sodium, saturated fat, chemical compounds derived from cellulose and additives. Undoubtedly, these burgers are huge mind-changers for people and are thus an important step in the right direction, but to call them veggie burgers may be stretching it a little as they don't have much to do with vegetables pulled straight from the ground.

After all, both these meatless burgers are made in laboratories. A Beyond Burger has 22 ingredients and contains just under 300 calories, 20g of industrially processed pea protein, just shy of 20g of fat, and nearly 400mg of salt.

My goal with this book is to teach you about the health benefits of a plant-based diet by making you more conscious of what you eat and the content of the food you eat. Therefore, it is only right to let you in on the truth, and the fact is that popular meat alternatives are not always full of healthy vegetables and should be eaten in moderation. Challenge yourself to taste the difference by eating a wholesome vegetable burger made from mushrooms, chickpeas, lentils or beans next time you are at a restaurant. Even if they have a tasty Beyond Burger on the menu, go natural and order the veggie burger instead. Know that you get natural protein from unprocessed ingredients that provide plenty of nutrition and are easily digestible – and they contain less fat, less sugar and less salt. Good for you!

Anyway: three cheers to all the meat-free choices you make!

today's task

There are ten days left of your 28 days vegan, and you have learned a lot! Take your new knowledge seriously and continue preparing food without ready-made meat replacements. It's time to tighten up on the use of processed products now. As we are entering the last part of the plan, there is no longer room for ready-made foods on the plate.

Remember to take notice of your daily wellbeing, and even better yet, pen it down in your diary or in the back of the book. Many people struggle with belly ache or feel bloated after eating bread, soy and pasta – without thinking about the connection. Are you among those who tend to feel drowsy after meals, maybe even need a nap? Since gut health has become such a popular topic recently, allow me to ask how your digestion is these days?

Switching to a plant-based diet has proven to be a very effective method of reducing gut disorders, as well as for losing weight. It becomes even more effective if you choose carefully what you put into your shopping cart. Avoid processed products that contain sugar, wheat flour, gluten and soy protein. Stay away from foods that contain ingredients that you cannot pronounce or ingredients that have names with numbers and letters.

Practise your new plant-based culinary skills inspired by the recipes and methods in this book. Avoid vegetarian mince and convenience foods. Tofu and tempeh are easy choices and are okay to cook for dinner once or twice a week. Cut two or three different vegetables into uniform sizes and stir-fry them. Or try steam-frying by adding a splash of water to the pan after a quick stir-fry, and cover with a lid to trap the steam inside. And roasted root vegetables are always hearty and delicious. Also remember that you do not need pasta, rice or potatoes on the plate for dinner. Replace with sweet potatoes, lentils, legumes, quinoa or black wild rice. This is especially important if you want to lose weight.

the domino effect

You are on a journey into the unknown, where you test boundaries and challenge your dietary habits. Certain foods are easy to remove from your shopping list, others you resist letting go. Occasionally, you may have looked the other way and ordered vegetarian when you're out with friends, or just couldn't find anything vegan on the menu. Or maybe you are among those who go 'all in' and will go on to become 100 per cent vegan, and will even avoid wearing leather and other products that contain traces of animals, such as glue and gelatin. By the way, did you know that most sweets contain gelatin made from pigs? A good reason to decline those gummy bears, if you ask me!

How relaxed or strict you are, or 'grow up' to be, will vary and change. Be patient, both with yourself and with those around you. Because you will – whether you want to or not – influence friends and others in your social circle. You will talk about your new eating plan. And friends will ask. Some will be a bit cautious, others more critical. Becoming vegan, whether for 28 days or for life, does not go by unnoticed. Common issues that freshly baked vegans face are how to refuse your mother-in-law's Sunday steak or what to do at friends' dinner parties where everyone eats everything.

Be aware that the pendulum has turned and it is no longer rude to say no thank you to a plate of meat. Never before have so many people been curious about vegan food, and it is trendy to be a conscious consumer. More and more people are becoming flexitarian, with meat ending up as the last alternative. If you say that you are vegan, you will often be greeted with a nod and a supportive story from the person next to you who would love to share their own new-found plant-based eating habits. You are a role model. It sounds overwhelming and a bit awkward, but that is the case. Every time you end up in a situation where your choice to be vegan elicits a response, it's a nudge on that person's conscience. This may not always be evident during your conversation, but you can be sure that it leaves them thinking.

Many people are on stand-by to reduce their meat consumption, as they are concerned and worried about their health, and some are even guilt-ridden because of environmental or animal rights issues. There are vegans who have seen friends run after the waiter to withdraw their order of a beef burger, and replace it with a veggie burger instead. Now, that's what I call positive influence.

Another thing is the domino effect on your own behaviour. It is only natural that your plant-based preferences will slip into other parts of life – not only your diet. After a while, some vegans gradually update their ideals and values, and with that awakens a stronger attitude to both environmental issues and animal ethics.

Dare to be an enthusiastic inspiration to your friends!

Next time you're invited to dinner, don't be afraid to reveal that you're vegan now. Offer to come earlier and create a plant-based side dish that fits the menu. Or why not bring your own Buddha bowl, and a generous amount so that curious guests also get to taste? Be thoughtful to your hosts, and use discretion to decide which dinner party is best suited for a vegan contribution. My experience is that both family and friends find it exciting with a few vegan sides on the table.

celebrity vegans

Being vegan is hot! The list of international celebrities who follow a plant-based diet is long. Here are some influential people who inspire others to become herbivores.

Alanis Morissette, *musician*
Alec Baldwin, *actor*
Alicia Silverston, *actor*
Anthony Kiedis, Red Hot Chili Peppers, *musician*
Ariana Grande, *artist*
Benedict Cumberbatch, *actor*
Bill Clinton, *ex-president*
Billie Eilish, *pop star*
Brad Pitt, *actor*
Bryan Adams, *musician*
Demi Moore, *actor*
Ellen Page, *actor*
Ellie Goulding, *musician*
Jared Leto, *actor and musician*
Jay-Z and Beyoncé, *musicians*
Jennifer Lopez, *actor and artist*
Jessica Chastain, *actor*
Jessica Simpson, *actor*
Joaquin Phoenix, *actor and vegan from early childhood*
Kat von D, *TV star*
Kate and Rooney Mara, *actors*

Lea Michele, *Glee actor*
Leona Lewis, *singer*
Lewis Hamilton, *Formula One star*
Liam Hemsworth, *actor*
Madonna, *artist*
Michelle Pfeiffer, *actor*
Moby, *musician*
Natalie Portman, *actor*
Pamela Anderson, *actor*
Petra Nemcova, *supermodel*
Portia de Rossi, *actor*
Russell Brand, *actor and musician*
Sia, *artist*
Stevie Wonder, *artist*
Venus and Serena Williams, *tennis champions*
Will.i.am, Black Eyed Peas, *musician*
Woody Harrelson, *actor*

ps.

A bonus for all you *Game of Thrones* fans: half the cast for GOT are vegans! Saluting Peter Dinklage (Tyrion Lannister), Maisie Williams (Arya Stark), Jerome Flynn (Bronn), Lena Headey (Cersei Lannister), Nathalie Emmanuel (Missandei), Bella Ramsey (Lyanna Mormont) and John Bradley (Samwell Tarly)!

animal-rights movies and documentaries worth your while

Cowspiracy (2014)
On the impact of industrial agriculture and meat production from an environmental perspective.

What the Health (2017)
About the health benefits of a plant-based diet. The film highlights the collaboration between the meat industry and the pharmaceutical industry.

Forks Over Knives (2011)
A controversial documentary that promotes a plant-based diet as a way to reverse lifestyle diseases.

Game Changers (2018)
A documentary by Oscar-winner James Cameron about the benefits of a plant-based diet for athletes.

Okja (2017)
About a friendly giant who becomes a puppet figure between cynical companies and animal keepers, and the girl who raised her. A critical look at the ethics of science.

Eating Animals (2017)
The adaption of Jonathan Safran Foer's book *Eating Animals*. About industrial animal farming and the food habits of the Western world.

Dominion (2018)
Award-winning documentary using drones and hidden cameras to reveal what is happening behind closed doors in the meat industry and in modern agriculture.

today's task

Watch one of the documentaries in the list above. Explore vegan influencers and add actors Joaquin Phoenix and Alicia Silverstone to your Instagram feed. And while you're at it, add Russell Brand too.

flex that culinary muscle

Today your only task is to exercise your new culinary skills. Cook a meal from scratch and serve it with a side dish that you haven't tried before.

Browse the food pictures in this book and choose something based on what you already have in your kitchen cabinets.

If you missed doing some of the tasks from the previous days, look through the book to recap. You have one week left of this vegan programme, and I promise you will get maximum payout when you take some time to reflect on how your journey has been so far.

Have you experienced change of any kind? Have you gained more energy, lost weight, or caught yourself talking about your new eating habits at work?

Or did you take a break and now you are reading this book with some detachment? Come on, jump back in again!

are you reading this book with some detachment? it's time to jump in!

a true friend

This is your last week of 28 days as a vegan, and you have every reason to be proud of yourself. Well done!

You've been through a lot these past three weeks. How do you feel about yourself? If you were to tell a close friend or partner – right now – how you feel, what would you say? And what did you note down in your diary yesterday? Am I right to guess that you get up with a little more drive in the morning? Are you sleeping a little better than before? Has your digestion improved? Do you experience a sense of wellbeing and less mood swings? Have you hit your target weight already, or have you slimmed down noticeably? You now know the connection between results and effort, having written a diary every day. Continue this conscious awareness and look at everything you eat and how it makes you feel.

As I am about to let go of your hand and see you off on your own, I want to make sure you remain a good friend to those around you. Your new eating preferences have probably already been the topic of conversation among your circle of friends and acquaintances, but now you will move into top gear: it's time to invite friends home for vegan food! We want you out of the closet. Show yourself: the vegan friend. And the best way to be a true friend is, of course, by sharing a good homemade meal. It is a great pleasure for vegans to invite people home for food. And an inspiration. Believe me, your friends are more interested than ever in what is cooking in your kitchen. Yes, most likely you'll get a lot more questions about what's for dinner than you are used to.

Remember that not everyone can, or will, keep up with the new direction your diet is taking you. The fact that you are now eating differently and more consciously than before will likely be affecting some of your friends' confidence because it forces them to look at their own plate and their own habits. Be generous and allow your friends to be both sceptical and critical of your choices. Just tell them how good you feel and invite them home for dinner!

today's task

Send a message to a friend and invite her or him to make a vegetable dish from this book one evening this week!

vegan on a budget

Now you know that no measuring cup, weighing scales or special ingredients are necessary to cook plant-based dishes. All you need is your choice of vegetables, a handful of herbs, a variety of plant milks, beans and lentils. Add a lemon, olive oil and a smile, too. I have already introduced you to the value of shopping in world food stores instead of your usual supermarket. Nuts, for example, tend to be quite expensive, but buying in bulk is often much cheaper. At the same stores you'll find chia seeds, flaxseeds, hemp seeds and sesame seeds. Not only are these tiny seeds packed full of protein and nutrition, they will add flavour and crunch to all vegan meals. You could also try buying nuts and seeds online for even better value. Shopping in expensive health food stores should be the exception and not the rule.

It is part of a vegan mindset to know the value of food, by paying attention to its content and origin, as well as being sustainably conscious in everyday life. This means, among other things, to save leftovers and don't over-serve food at home.

Since Day 17, I know that you have already changed your attitude to food waste and you have started practising smart things like planning menus with leftovers in mind; at the very least you're eating yesterday's dinner for lunch the next day. You've learned a few tricks to keep vegetables fresh and crisp for longer.

Eating plant-based is easily cheaper than a standard meat-eating diet. The secret to saving money on food is first and foremost about how you treat the raw materials. It's like the roses in the fairy tale *The Little Prince*, where the little prince shows you how it is

the watering and caring of the singled-out favourite rose that will make it more precious to you. Same thing with home cooking: when you spend more time cooking vegetables and sharing love through the food you serve, this will automatically lead you to start taking better care of leftovers. And by all means you want to avoid throwing leftovers in the bin. It gradually becomes natural to put your leftovers in airtight containers and store them in the fridge for the next day.

Proper food storage and using everything you have in the fridge and the kitchen cabinets go hand in hand. You just don't throw away withered veggies. You put them in a bowl of water and leave them overnight in the fridge. The next day they are just as nice and fresh, and an excellent dinner ingredient. Be sure to buy tinned chopped tomatoes and lentils in bulk instead of expensive ready-made pasta sauces.

Check the fridge before you go to the shops. Let the contents of your fridge and kitchen cabinets decide what will be for dinner for the next few days — using what you have is the absolute safest way to reduce your food budget.

Make your own sandwiches at home for lunch and splurge on spreads and sprouts rather than buying expensive plastic-wrapped lunches from a high-street chain. Don't forget to bring along one of those homemade lunches next time you travel or are on the go. It is just a healthier and more sustainable way of eating. And cheaper!

The truth is that both meat and fish are more expensive than vegetables and legumes, so you will always save money on a plant-based diet. If you follow my advice in this book, you will save money!

today's task

Make a full inventory of the food contents of your kitchen. When you started this programme 23 days ago, I asked you to do the same thing. Since then, you have likely bought new foods, and you have certainly eaten your previous supplies. Therefore, take another look and note what you have. Again, my main goal is to teach you to think of vegetables in the context of balanced meals. So link the contents of your cabinets to actual meals. Look at the tins of chopped tomatoes and imagine how you could use them in something that tastes good: pasta sauce, lasagne sauce, tomato soup and pizza sauce are obvious suggestions. Look for packets of chickpeas and decide to make hummus today or tomorrow. Or make the Garlic-Roasted Chickpeas and Carrots on page 138. If you have beetroots, cook them and use two for beet hummus and the rest in a delicious salad or as a sandwich filling. Do this for each food item as you go through your cabinets. This will not only make you aware of what you have and limit your shopping list, it will also teach you how to connect foods with specific meals. Don't buy more food than you need for the coming week.

travelling and on the go

A major obstacle for many who are beginners at plant-based eating is they can't find anything healthy to eat when they are travelling.

The healthy food options in petrol stations and airports are often few and far between. You are left with baguettes with a pile of butter, cheese sandwiches, pizza Margherita and chips – and let's face it, these are mostly junk food. High-carb food that quickly turns into sugar in your body.

Not only can you put on weight, this kind of food leaves you feeling tired, bloated and irritated. Mood swings are a common result of the excessive sugar content in 'white' and high-carb foods.

One of the most important things I want you to know as you continue your plant-based journey in the future is this: travelling doesn't have to limit you as a vegan. It only takes a little preparation before you go. In return, you should save money, keep your good spirits, stay in shape and keep your ideal weight!

Tips to stay on a steady, healthy vegan course while travelling:

· Make lunch to go at home. Use brown bread, try sourdough made of spelt, spread on your favourite topping, add your favourite filling. Wrap in vegan wrap or baking parchment. Put in your travel bag. Boom. Finished. You'll be walking past all the kiosks and delis with white carbs on display while looking forward to eating your delicious homemade lunch.

· A banana, a small bag of nuts and two carrots will sustain you nicely on a long road trip and then some, before landing in time for dinner at your destination.

· Flights will never be the same after you first pre-order a vegan meal. All airline companies offer so-called 'special meals' which you can easily book online. I promise, the little meal the flight attendant brings you, before they start tending to everyone else, is way healthier than the white bread, over-cooked pasta or soft piece of pizza everyone else on board gets. Notice the envious glances from your fellow passengers.

· At the hotel, make sure to tell the staff at the reception check-in that you are vegan, and ask them to find local dinner options for you. And, of course, let the waiting staff at the hotel restaurant know, and don't be surprised when they offer you something extra for your breakfast plate in the morning.

Remember what you learned on Day 5 about being in a restaurant: you can have it your way. Ask waiters, flight attendants and receptionists if they can help you find something to eat.

today's task

Avoid the fruit yoghurts, ice creams, Frappuccinos and sugary pre-made ice lattes if you make a pit stop at a service station. Take a closer look at the shelves and ask the staff if they have any veggie options – cold or warm. Some service stations serve vegan burgers, which will work fine if you forgot to pack a lunch. And I confess that I have a weak service-station spot – sweet potato fries.

ps.

Fill up a glass bottle with refreshing lemon water (simply squeeze in a few slices of lemon) at home, so you don't have to buy expensive water in plastic bottles!

for the men

The upsurge in the number of vegans across Europe and the US has been well documented and covered in the media. With the continuous concerns about animal welfare and the global environment, a study by finder.com (UK diet trends 2020) indicates the number of vegans is set to rise steeply in the UK over the next year.

However, the figures show that the number of vegan women is much higher than the number of men. In the UK, according to a study conducted by the Vegan Society in 2016, 63 per cent of those who define themselves as vegans are women, compared to just 37 per cent men. In the US, 79 per cent of vegans are women. Perhaps we can't necessarily assume that it's like this everywhere, but if you are a vegan man, you can congratulate yourself!

The reason I look at this is because it turns out that women are often the most important target group for all types of dietary changes. Why are women more likely to be vegan than men? Perhaps there is still a masculine culture of males bonding over a cheese burger and a beer. But the fact is, men have everything to gain by eating less meat.

Just listen to this:

Meat contains saturated fat, which raises blood cholesterol levels, which in turn is a risk factor for heart disease. Health experts also warn that a high consumption of sugar and 'fast' carbs increases the risk of developing type 2 diabetes, which escalates the risk of developing heart disease. This means that steak, cheese burgers and too much convenience food that contains sugar and starch will clog blood vessels — both in men and women. As we know that it's mostly men who are affected by cardiovascular disease, it is logical that men, too, would benefit from a vegan diet. Narrowed blood vessels and arteries not only weaken the heart, it also means poor blood circulation to other vital organs. Impotence can be an early sign of cardiovascular disease. Plants, including fermented plants, are full of fibre, lactic acid bacteria and polyphenols (a group of phytonutrients) that can help reduce inflammation and prevent cardiovascular disease, and thus strengthen the heart and increase sexual potency.

Gradually it became socially accepted that to quit smoking would improve health. Ask any man at the gym and he'll agree that exercise also improves health, even at a very moderate level. Do we dare claim that a plant-based diet may be the 'missing link' in this picture? Will we see a decline in heart disease if far more men reduced their meat intake in favour of vegetables? It's an interesting thought.

Switching to a plant-based diet will also be a smart choice if you want to lose weight. Three out of four Norwegian men suffer from obesity, according to the Norwegian Institute of Public Health (the figure for women was not as high). Obesity in the UK has been creeping upwards since 2000. Nutritional physiologists agree that what is beneficial for the health of men is also beneficial from an environmental perspective: the answer is more plant-based eating, and less processed red meat and sugar. It is well documented that a plant-based diet, and especially a vegan one, can help protect against obesity. A good enough reason to go on a meat detox, isn't it? In fact, my experience is that both men and women who go all in and follow my advice in this book can lose up to 3–5 kilos during their 28 days as a vegan (depending on their starting point).

A high intake of processed meat can also affect male fertility. According to research, men who eat a lot of meat and dairy products may have fewer and slower sperm than their plant-eating friends. Spinach, asparagus, broccoli and tomatoes are said to be beneficial for male fertility. Maybe this could serve as a gentle green nudge for couples who want to start a family?

Your mental health is also connected to what you eat. Research has shown that eating fresh fruits and vegetables, oats, wild rice, nuts and seeds is a good countermeasure to mood swings. Eating comfort food is not uncommon when we're feeling down. So reducing our meat consumption could really help us achieve two things in one single action: reducing obesity as well as curbing mild depression.

Finally, an inspirational case from one of our favourite vegans, the American actor Woody Harrelson. When he was in his early twenties, he was bothered by bad skin breakouts. One day he sat next to a stranger on the bus who urged him to cut out all dairy products. According to the stranger, Woody should start to notice great improvement in three days. Woody Harrelson never looked back after experiencing the positive results of this advice.

I could go on and on, but I'll just share one more example. I have to mention a great sportsman – and vegan – the American Rich Roll, winner of the Ultraman endurance challenge and many times triathlon winner. He was a 40-year-old couch potato with a beer in one hand and a burger in the other when he suffered a midlife crisis – and so he changed his diet and lifestyle from one day to the next. He has made his greatest sports achievements as a vegan, and today he is a great inspiration to many athletes – both meat eaters and vegans. Check out his podcast for inspiration!

pep-talk and one final push

You haven't eaten meat or dairy in almost four weeks, and like most others, you probably think it has been easier than you anticipated.

Some things you thought were going to be hard have been easy beyond all expectation. In fact, you've even thought that being vegan is pretty cool. Now you know how it feels. Whether you embarked on this journey simply because you wanted inspiration on how to eat more vegetables, or you wanted to slim down a little, or you needed an energy boost in your life, there's a big chance you've reached your goal. Provided you followed the plan and all the advice in this book, it's likely you have felt a powerful change and an improvement in your wellbeing. Be aware, this is a major lifestyle change. It is only natural that you notice a difference in your body or mind after almost four weeks. But if you haven't, take a timeout today. Read through your diary. Reflect on the days that have passed and what you have learned, thought, experienced and known to be true during the past four weeks. After all the effort you put into these weeks, you deserve to finish with style.

Often, motivation has a tendency to fizzle out bit by bit after a period of much enthusiasm. Just think of everyone who joins a gym in January and starts off with great zeal. Towards the end of January or, at best, February, many find that they have returned to their old routines and have more or less stopped exercising. Yoyo dieting is a result of the same thought patterns — you jump into a diet with strict goals and courageous efforts, only to put the kilos back on again when the plan is over and you are back to everyday life. I want you to succeed at a higher level than that. I want you to take home all your new knowledge of wholesome ingredients and food contents. I hope you have learned to see the connections between food and how it makes you feel. Perhaps most of all I want you to take with you what you have learned about looking at vegetables as a meal in themselves. That you have started cooking with vegetables as the main ingredient with the examples given in this book. That you've used sweet potato, full of beta-carotene and less starch than regular potatoes (boiled white potatoes in fact contain almost twice the amount of starch than boiled sweet potatoes). That you've tried sliced radish in your sandwich or mixed in salads. You've scrubbed beets and oven-baked them. You've tasted plant-based milks instead of cow's milk, either oat or almond, and you've started ordering your coffee latte with oat milk as standard. You've realised that you can do without dairy and yoghurt, and you have replaced cheese and ham on your pizza and in your sandwich with plant-based alternatives. Hummus and vegan mayonnaise are your new besties and an accessory to almost everything you eat, and you use fresh herbs and sprouts to spice it up a little here, there and everywhere.

No matter how much you take with you from this 28-day plan, I am pretty sure that these weeks have given you irreversible experiences and discoveries. Most people are not 100 per cent vegan though, as you have been for almost four weeks now — if you have followed closely every day. You do not need to continue a plant-based diet if you do not want to. That said, don't give up until it's over. You still have a few days left. Let Olympic cross-country skier Therese Johaug or champion distance runner Jakob Ingebrigtsen inspire you with their extraordinary capability to give their last 100 per cent in the very final crucial moments before the finish line. Or better yet, British vegan runner Fiona Oakes who holds several world marathon records for running. She knows a thing or two about stamina.

Review everything you have experienced and learned and use it actively daily. Don't celebrate until it's over. If you weighed yourself when you started, keep an eye on the scale. Did you not achieve your goals? Think about what you have eaten. Be honest. If you have taken one too many shortcuts with ready-made meals, you may have consumed a lot of fast-release carbohydrates and too much sugar. If, on the other hand, you have eaten mostly vegetables for lunch and dinner, you may be experiencing a refreshing feeling of lightness in your body and mind.

Now there's only two days left. Let the last days be TOTALLY plant-based. The results are right in front of you.

today's task

Take 30 minutes me-time and sit down on the floor. Make a little extra room for yourself, and get into a lotus position if you can. Or settle on a kitchen chair with a straight back and feet well planted on the floor. Close your eyes and think about what you've been through. Maybe you want to read your food diary before you sit down. Use this as an opportunity to contemplate everything you've learned, all the new green stuff you've eaten, and how you've been these past weeks.

Decide for yourself that you will be completely free of ready-made meals for the next few days. Avoid foods with sugar and wheat, like waffles, cakes and white bread and rolls as much as you can. And please don't eat your dinner too late at night. Resolve to drink only herbal tea in the evening and eat no food after dinner. Remember what you wanted when you started this. What were your goals and which health benefits were you looking for? This is it, the deadline is close now.

are you cheating?

Have you been wanting to cheat during the past month? It is perfectly normal if you have. As I said at the beginning, it takes time to change habits. You may be tempted to give up on your newfound healthy ways, even if you are so close to reaching the end of your meatless month. Occasionally, the craving for sweets may just be too much to handle, or your willpower too weak and the sweet memories of cakes too strong to resist your favourite bakeries. Know this: this too will pass. If you only knew what a few more weeks of a conscious awareness of sugar, sweetened dairy products and butter- or cream-based sauces and dressings, would do for you. You will notice that the craving and longing for sweets and snacks is soon gone. Your taste buds will gradually adapt to your healthy diet, and eventually you will — believe it or not — come to find that sweets, cakes, fruit yoghurts and chocolate snacks taste almost nasty.

What you have experienced already, or are about to experience, is perhaps one of the best things about a plant-based diet: you get to fill up on slow-release carbs and eat a balanced diet that keeps your blood sugar under control. The result is you completely forget to think about snacking in-between meals simply because your body doesn't

need it. Again, it is easier to keep your ideal weight if you stick to your main meals and stay away from high-calorie snacks throughout the day.

I'm not condemning all convenience foods or vegan meat or even the occasional cheese snack. I don't even look down on sugary stuff like cookies, cakes and pastries. However, you are about to find out that there is no need for cheating, because this type of food no longer has much appeal. There is so much good food to be had. All plant-based. Of course, we all have our guilty pleasures. Chips, for example. Chips are my vice. Now, choose your favourite plant-based guilty pleasure and stick to it. At the same time decide that your old vices and snacks are not on the menu any more. So many people say to me: 'Oh, this vegan journey has truly been fun and easier than I had anticipated, but I am NOT going to continue eating fully plant-based.' To all of you I say: If you think you can't continue your plant-based vegan diet, then choose one day of the week when you can eat meat, and eat plant-based the other days. Or, if it suits you better, decide to eat vegan dinners every single day, and have a little piece of meat for lunch if you must. These are all little measures that will make a big difference to your life.

Be an ambassador for vegan living and share your experiences with the Facebook group Greenstuff.no and follow me @lailamadso on Instagram. In addition, your own feed on social media is a good place to spread positive vibes about the benefits you have gained on your meatless journey.

completed & let's celebrate!

Congratulations! You have completed the programme and been vegan for 28 days! We will celebrate with delicious party food.

Now you might want to breathe out and celebrate that it's over. Obviously you should celebrate. But put one foot steadily on the ground before heading off to your local restaurant to order your old favourite dishes. Please continue to be conscious about what you put in your mouth, even if you want to have cheese or sushi on the menu again. Your new plant-based diet is not controlled by a vegan judge who sits in your fridge and decides what you do with your life. One of the goals of this book is to get you used to the connection between what you eat and how you feel. The health aspect is one thing. But maybe you have a new view on greenhouse gas emissions linked to the food industry? Maybe you have started reading more news articles about global climate change?

Keep it up! This is a sign that something has happened. To YOU. At the beginning of this book, we talked about the fact that something has happened to the world. Now you are a bigger part of it than you were 28 days ago. Receive it with open arms. As a human being you are the sum of all your experiences. Remember what it was that first made you want to go on this vegan journey, and apply your new knowledge and experiences to your life now. For example, if

you haven't already, join my Facebook group Greenstuff.no, where past passengers on the *How To Be Vegan in 28 Days* journey give their tips and opinions about plant-based stuff.

There is no need to ease off now. On the contrary, see this as your great opportunity to introduce your inner circle to what you have learned over the past month. Yesterday's task was to be a vegan ambassador and spread positive vibes. Yes, that's what you've been up to if you've been following the plan all month. Now you know what a plant-based lifestyle is all about and why it is singled out as the best way to contribute to a better global climate. Spreading a positive message about plant-based eating can be a huge contribution to your friends' health, to the planet and to animal welfare. Try to meet all curious questions with patience. Know that even the most critical person will take notice. In some, the interest is hidden with scepticism. It's okay. Invite them over to your house for a vegan dinner party!

Let them know in advance that you will serve a plant-based menu and I bet your friends will be extra interested and accept the invitation with great curiosity.

Just remember: be kind to yourself. Vegans are not ascetics. We are pleasure-seekers and people who enjoy life! We celebrate life and longevity by eating wholefoods, and try as best we can to live sustainably. This means, among other things, that many of us are more than happy to enjoy a glass of red wine and a piece of dark chocolate after dinner. If you don't fancy the bitterness of dark chocolate (which is full of healthy antioxidants), there are many different types of delicious vegan chocolate made from sweeter-tasting plant milks.

Back to our celebration. Today is a reason to show some love! Make a little extra effort with your vegan feast, even if it's just for you, or if you invite only one friend. Buy a vegan cookbook for inspiration, or find encouragement on social media among the many wonderfully tempting dishes shown there. Keep cooking the dishes from this book.

As a tip, I recommend making many small dishes and serving them as a tapas-style buffet.

Here is a list of ideas for your vegan tapas menu selected from this book:
— Make four varieties of hummus and serve with sourdough bread or chips, see page 151.
— Vegan Aioli, see page 157.
— Three types of snacks, see page 161.
— Make a large bowl of Fried Rice with Edamame, Mushrooms and Carrots, see page 142.
— Cauliflower Rice with Quinoa, Tomatoes, Crispy Seeds and Hummus, see page 98.
— Falafel with Pickled Onions and Coconut Yoghurt, see page 134.

These vegan waffles are always a success. The combination of salty and sweet is so good! Everyone is going to ask you about the recipe, which, by the way, is the easiest ever. The photo is from the Instagram account @veganeri28dager where you can find inspiration for your 28-day vegan journey.

Vegan waffles

200g wholegrain spelt flour
1 tsp baking powder
1 tsp Ceylon cinnamon
½ tsp salt
450ml oat or almond milk
100ml aquafaba
1 x 400g tin of white beans, any type
2 tbsp plant-based margarine

Use a hand blender to mix all the ingredients together into a smooth batter. Leave for 10–15 minutes. Whisk again for 10 seconds and cook in either a preheated waffle iron or a hot, dry frying pan. Serve with salty spreads and toppings or make a sweet dessert topped with coconut, blueberries and vegan parmesan. Sprinkle with some sea salt, if possible black charcoal salt for the colour.

17 hearty dinners

All recipes serve 3–4

Veggie dishes that save the world! This is the food you can live on for the rest of the month – and, yes, the rest of the year, if you ask me. All dishes are made from one of these main ingredients: squash, cauliflower, broccoli, carrot, cabbage, sweet potato, lentils, celeriac and chickpeas. These 17 recipes are easy to follow and contain few ingredients. At the same time, the idea is that you can swap the ingredients in many of the recipes – if you're missing one ingredient, you simply use another. And please, no need to be super specific with the amounts in most of these recipes, the whole idea is that you can increase or reduce the amounts as you like. I call it freestyle cooking! Have a nice drink, put on some good music, and enjoy practising your new culinary skills. Combine your meal with one or two of your favourite vegan weapons – and, most importantly, flirt with your guests. As a bonus, I'll give you the recipe for a spice mix that makes your vegetables even more exciting.

you're welcome!

cauliflower

Cauliflower risotto with capers, herb oil and raw marinated cauliflower

2 cauliflowers
olive oil
juice of 1 lemon
sea salt
4 shallots, finely chopped
2 garlic cloves, finely chopped
200g risotto rice
2 litres vegetable broth
pinch of ground cayenne pepper
Green Herb Oil (see page 147)
2 tbsp capers

Cut the cauliflowers into florets, set aside the largest florets for marinating. Bring a large pan of lightly salted water to the boil and put the rest of the cauliflower in to cook for about 10 minutes, or until tender. Drain, reserving a mug of the cooking water, and purée the cauliflower in a blender. Add a little of the cooking water to thin it down if necessary.

Thinly slice the reserved cauliflower florets with a sharp knife or use a mandolin for easy slicing. Toss the slices in a little olive oil and lemon juice, with a pinch of salt.

Heat a little oil in a pan over a medium heat and sauté the shallots and garlic for 5 minutes until glossy. Stir in the risotto rice, then little by little add the vegetable broth whilst the rice gently simmers, stirring frequently. When the rice is al dente after about 30 minutes, it is ready. Mix in the cauliflower purée. Season with salt, lemon juice and a pinch of cayenne pepper.

Serve the risotto with some of the herb oil, capers and the raw marinated cauliflower.

Cauliflower rice with quinoa, tomatoes, crispy seeds and hummus

2 cauliflowers
100g red or white quinoa
4 tbsp pumpkin seeds
4 tbsp sunflower seeds
100ml extra virgin olive oil, plus a little extra
6 tomatoes, preferably in different sizes and colours
pinch of fennel seeds, crushed in a mortar
pinch of coriander seeds, crushed in a mortar
sea salt
juice of 1 lemon
Hummus (see page 151)

Remove any leaves from the cauliflowers. Cut the cauliflowers into large chunks, then roughly grate into rice using a box grater, or you could use a food processor.

Cook the quinoa according to the packet instructions, then drain. Fry the pumpkin and sunflower seeds in a little oil until golden and crispy. Cut the tomatoes into wedges.

Put the cauliflower rice, quinoa, tomatoes, spices and the rest of the olive oil into a bowl, then season with salt and lemon juice. Spread a thin layer of hummus onto a plate and add the cauliflower mixture. Top it all with a sprinkle of crispy seeds.

Option: sauté the cauliflower rice in a large frying pan over a medium heat for a few minutes before serving with hummus.

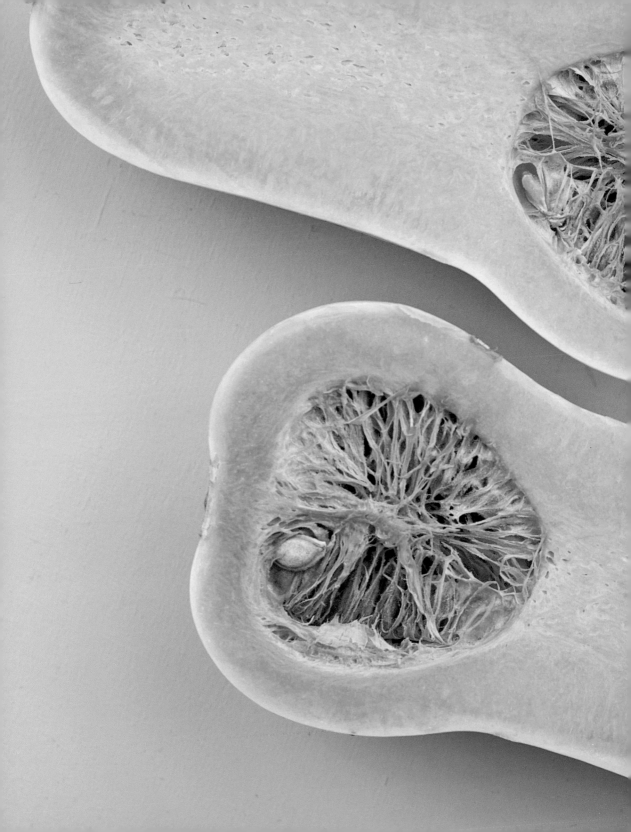

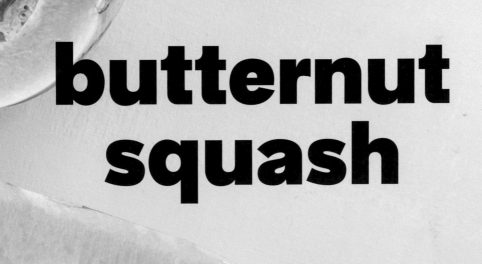

butternut squash

Roasted butternut squash with quinoa, kale and crispy pumpkin seeds

1 butternut squash
olive oil
2 garlic cloves, roughly chopped
pinch of sea salt
100g pumpkin seeds
200g kale, stems removed, leaves roughly chopped
juice of 1 lemon
200g red quinoa
pumpkin seed oil
Vegan Mayonnaise (see page 157) or Vegan Aioli (see page 157),
to serve

Preheat the oven to 180°C/160°C fan/gas mark 4.

Peel the butternut squash and remove the seeds, then cut into large cubes. Toss in a little olive oil and the garlic, along with a pinch of salt, then roast in the oven for 20 minutes until tender. Pan-fry the pumpkin seeds in a little oil until golden and crispy, and then fold in the chopped kale. Season with salt and lemon juice.

Cook the quinoa according to the packet instructions, then drain. Spoon the squash, kale and pumpkin seeds on top of the quinoa and drizzle over a little pumpkin seed oil, or olive oil. Serve with mayonnaise or aioli.

Red Thai curry with butternut squash, coconut milk, lime and wild rice

200g wild rice, presoaked
1 butternut squash
rapeseed oil
2 tbsp red curry paste
4 lime leaves, dried or fresh
6 mushrooms, thinly sliced
2 shallots, finely chopped
1 stick of lemon grass, finely chopped
1 red chilli, finely chopped
1 x 400ml tin of coconut milk
sea salt
juice of 1 lime
1 bunch of coriander, roughly chopped

Cook the wild rice in a 1:3 rice to water ratio for about 45 minutes.

Meanwhile, peel the squash and remove the seeds, then cut into cubes. Heat a little rapeseed oil in a pan over a medium heat and fry the curry paste and lime leaves for a couple of minutes. Add the squash, mushrooms, shallots, lemon grass and chilli and fry for another minute. Add the coconut milk and cook for 20 minutes, or until the squash is tender. Season with salt and lime juice and scatter over the coriander. Serve the curry alongside the rice in a separate bowl.

cabbage

Cabbage salad with fennel, mango, pomegranate and fried quinoa

rapeseed oil
200g quinoa
1 pointed cabbage
1 savoy cabbage
2 fennel
100ml apple juice
½ tsp ground cumin
2 pinches of sea salt
1 ripe mango
1 pomegranate

Heat a good amount of rapeseed oil in a large pan over a medium heat and fry the quinoa for about 10 minutes, or until golden and crispy. Remove from the pan and set aside.

Remove any damaged leaves and the tough stalks from the cabbages and fennel, then cut them into strips. Heat a little oil in a pan over a medium heat and fry them for a minute or two. Add the apple juice, cumin and salt. Cook until the cabbage is tender and the apple juice has evaporated, about 10 minutes.

Peel and roughly chop the mango and remove the seeds from the pomegranate. Serve the cabbage and fennel mixture with the mango and pomegranate seeds on top and sprinkled with the crispy quinoa.

Grilled cabbage with miso dressing, pea purée, sunflower seeds and sprouts

2 white or pointed cabbages
rapeseed oil
4 tbsp Miso Dressing (see page 159)
sea salt
4 tbsp sunflower seeds
juice of 1 lemon
a handful of radish sprouts, or other sprouts
Pea Purée (see page 153), to serve

Remove the outer leaves from the cabbages and cut them in half lengthways. Drizzle the cut sides with rapeseed oil and a tablespoon of miso dressing and sprinkle with salt. Grill or pan-fry over a high heat until golden and tender, about 15 minutes. You may want to splash a little water into the pan to sauté it further.

Fry the sunflower seeds in a little oil until golden and crispy. Sprinkle lemon juice, the crispy sunflower seeds and sprouts over the cabbage. Serve with pea purée and more miso dressing.

broccoli

Broccoli and avocado wok with caramelised onion hummus, chilli and sprouts

1 broccoli head
2 avocados
rapeseed oil
2 garlic cloves, finely chopped
juice of 1 lemon
pinch of sea salt
pinch of chilli flakes
a handful of broccoli sprouts or other sprouts
Caramelised Red Onion Hummus (see page 151)

Cut off the broccoli stalk and peel it. Divide the broccoli into florets and roughly chop the stalk. Cut the avocados in half and remove the stone and peel. Slice the flesh lengthways. Heat a little rapeseed oil in a large frying pan or wok over a medium-high heat until smoking hot. Pan-fry the broccoli and avocado until golden, about 5 minutes. Towards the end, add the garlic, lemon juice and salt. To finish, sprinkle over the chilli flakes and sprouts. Serve with hummus.

Tenderstem broccoli and tofu in black bean sauce with cherry tomatoes and sesame seeds

400g firm tofu
rapeseed oil
200g tenderstem broccoli
12–15 red cherry tomatoes, cut in half
4 tbsp black bean sauce
2 tbsp water
juice of 1 lime
2 tbsp white sesame seeds, toasted

Cut the tofu into cubes. Heat a little rapeseed oil in a pan over a medium heat and fry the tofu for 5 minutes, or until golden. Carefully remove from the pan and set aside. Pan-fry the broccoli for a minute or so before adding the cherry tomatoes, the black bean sauce and water. Cook for 5 minutes, then season with lime juice. Sprinkle with sesame seeds and serve with the tofu.

celeriac

Celeriac steaks with crushed edamame, mushrooms and sriracha dressing

1 large celeriac or 2 small ones
coarse salt/sea salt
rapeseed oil
200g oyster mushrooms or cremini mushrooms
juice of 1 lime or lemon
400g edamame beans
2 green chillies, finely chopped
2 garlic cloves, finely chopped
extra virgin olive oil
Sriracha Dressing (see page 157), to serve

Preheat the oven to 180°C/160°C fan/gas mark 4.

Place the celeriac in a roasting tin with a generous layer of coarse salt/sea salt in the bottom and bake in the oven for about 1 hour, or until tender. Let the celeriac cool slightly before removing the skin with a sharp knife and cutting into thick steaks. Heat a little rapeseed oil in a pan over a medium heat and fry one side of the steaks for a few minutes until golden. Flip and cook for another few minutes. Remove from the pan, then fry the mushrooms in a little oil until golden and season with salt and lime or lemon juice.

Crush the edamame in a mortar, then add the chillies, garlic and a little olive oil. Season with a little more salt and lime or lemon juice. Serve the steaks with the crushed edamame and mushrooms on top and the sriracha dressing on the side.

sweet
potato

Salt-baked and grilled sweet potato with romaine lettuce, wild rice and walnuts

4 sweet potatoes
coarse salt/sea salt
200g wild rice, presoaked for a few hours or even overnight
olive oil
2 romaine lettuce hearts
4 tbsp Vegan Pesto (see page 149)
100g walnuts, coarsely chopped

Preheat the oven to 180°C/160°C fan/gas mark 4.

Place the sweet potatoes in a roasting tin with a generous layer of coarse salt in the bottom and bake in the oven for about 1 hour, or until tender.

Meanwhile, cook the wild rice in a 1:3 rice to water ratio for about 45 minutes. When the potatoes are done, allow to cool slightly before removing the skin and cutting in half lengthways. Drizzle over a little oil and grill or fry in a hot pan until golden and slightly crispy.

Divide the romaine lettuces into leaves. Arrange the sweet potatoes, rice and salad leaves on your plates. Spoon the pesto over the leaves and scatter over the walnuts before serving.

Tacos with five-spice fried sweet potato, avocado cream, pickled red onions and mango salsa

2 large sweet potatoes, peeled and cut into cubes
2 tbsp Five-Spice (see page 149)
rapeseed oil
2 ripe avocados
juice of 1 lime
1 bunch of coriander, chopped
sea salt
1 ripe mango, cut into cubes
seeds of 1 pomegranate
1 red chilli, finely chopped
extra virgin olive oil
12 corn tortilla wraps
Pickled Red Onions (see page 155)
Vegan Mayonnaise (see page 157)
1 lime, cut into quarters, to serve

Season the sweet potato cubes with five-spice. Heat a little rapeseed oil in a pan over a medium heat and fry the cubes for about 15–20 minutes until tender.

Make the avocado cream by cutting the avocados in half and removing the stone and peel. Blend the avocado, lime juice, half the coriander and a pinch of salt into a smooth cream.

Make the mango salsa by mixing the mango and pomegranate seeds in a bowl before adding the chilli and a little extra virgin olive oil along with the rest of the coriander.

To assemble, toast the tortillas slightly in a dry frying pan, top them with the avocado cream, sweet potato, mango salsa, pickled red onions and vegan mayonnaise. Serve with lime quarters.

legumes & pulses

Red lentil dhal with cumin, radishes, edamame and horseradish

rapeseed oil or olive oil
2 red onions, finely chopped
2 garlic cloves, finely chopped
500g dried red lentils
1 x 400g tin of chopped tomatoes
1 tbsp ground cumin
1 tbsp smoked paprika
1 litre vegetable broth
sea salt
juice of 1 lemon
200g edamame beans
4 radishes, thinly sliced
grated horseradish, to serve

Heat a little oil in a pan over a medium heat and sauté the onions for 5 minutes before adding the garlic. Cook for a couple more minutes. Add the lentils, tomatoes, spices and vegetable broth and simmer for about 20 minutes, or until the lentils are tender. Season with salt, a splash of lemon juice and, if necessary, more spices.

Toss the edamame and radish slices in a little rapeseed or olive oil and lemon juice, along with a pinch of salt, and spoon over the lentils. Serve with grated horseradish on top.

Falafel with pickled onions and coconut yoghurt

400g dried chickpeas, soaked overnight
4 garlic cloves
2 green chillies
1 bunch of coriander, leaves picked and stalks chopped
½ bunch of parsley
sea salt
2 pinches of ground cumin
juice of 2 lemons
rapeseed oil
coconut yoghurt, or oat crème fraîche, to serve
Pickled Red Onions (see page 155), to serve

Drain the chickpeas and rinse well. Roughly blitz in a food processor with the garlic, chillies and herbs (except the coriander stalks). Season with salt, cumin and lemon juice. Shape the mixture into balls of your desired size. Preferably chill for an hour in the fridge before cooking, so they keep their shape better.

Heat a little rapeseed oil in a pan over a medium-high heat and fry the falafel for about 10 minutes, turning frequently, until golden and cooked through. Mix the chopped coriander stalks with the coconut yoghurt. Serve with pickled red onions.

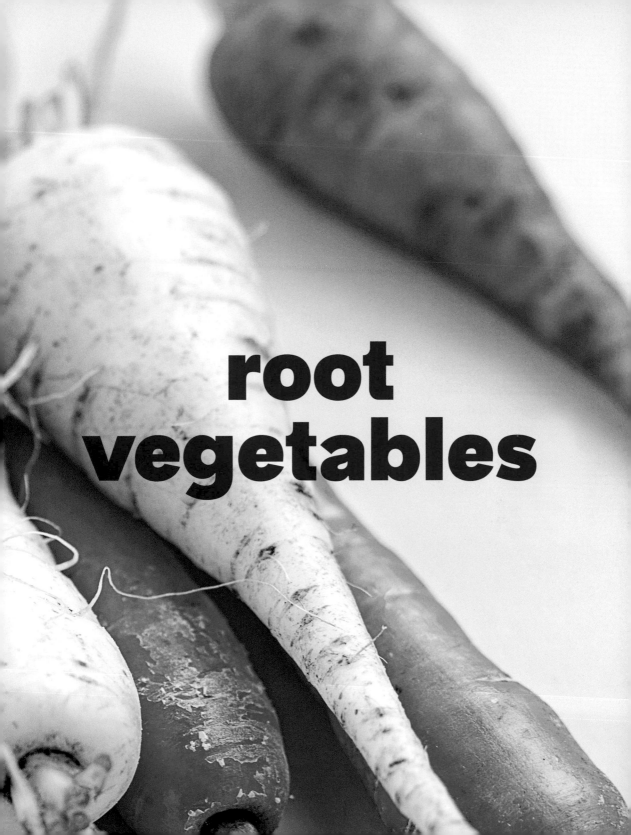

root vegetables

Garlic-roasted chickpeas and carrots with tahini dressing and herb quinoa

16 small carrots
300g dried chickpeas, soaked overnight
8 garlic cloves, unpeeled
pinch of ground cumin
4 tbsp rapeseed oil
2 pinches of salt, plus a little more to taste
200g white quinoa
100ml extra virgin olive oil
1 bunch of parsley, chopped
1 bunch of mint, chopped
juice of 1 lemon
Tahini Dressing (see page 159), to serve

Preheat the oven to 180°C/160°C fan/gas mark 4.

Scrub the carrots. Mix the carrots, chickpeas, garlic, cumin, rapeseed oil and salt in a roasting tin and roast in the oven for 30 minutes, or until tender.

Cook the quinoa according to the packet instructions, then drain. Mix in the olive oil and chopped herbs, then season with a little more salt and lemon juice, to taste. Serve with tahini dressing.

Salt-baked beets with beetroot hummus, chickpeas, spinach and hazelnuts

1 large beetroot
1 large yellow beetroot
coarse salt/sea salt
100g chickpeas, from a 400g tin
1 or 2 handfuls of baby spinach
extra virgin olive oil
juice of 1 lemon
Beetroot Hummus (see page 151)
100g hazelnuts, roughly chopped (optional)

Preheat the oven to 180°C/160°C fan/gas mark 4.

Place the beetroots in a roasting tin with a generous layer of coarse salt/sea salt in the bottom. Cover with foil (optional) and bake for about 1 hour, or until tender. Allow the beets to cool before removing the skins and dividing them into quarters.

Meanwhile, mix the chickpeas and spinach in a bowl. Toss them in olive oil and lemon juice, along with a pinch of salt. Spread some beetroot hummus onto a plate, place the beets on top and then add the chickpeas and spinach. Sprinkle with chopped hazelnuts, if desired.

Fried rice with edamame, mushrooms and carrots

150g wild rice, presoaked
1 tbsp sunflower oil
6 mushrooms, any kind you like, thinly sliced
1 garlic clove, finely chopped
3 tbsp edamame beans
4 spring onions, finely chopped
1 carrot, grated
2 tbsp tamari (or soy sauce), plus extra to serve (optional)
2 tbsp toasted sesame seeds
juice of 1 lemon
Miso Dressing (see page 159), to serve

Cook the wild rice in a 1:3 rice to water ratio for about 45 minutes.

Heat the oil in a pan over a medium heat and fry the mushrooms, garlic and edamame for 3 minutes. Add the cooked rice and continue to cook for 1 minute. Stir in the spring onions, grated carrot, tamari and sesame seeds and fry for a further minute. Season with lemon juice and pour over the miso dressing or a little extra tamari before serving, if you like.

23

vegan weapons

. . . a perfect fit with all your veggie dishes

Here you are! Twenty-three vegan weapons disguised as useful basic recipes for dressings, sauces, dips and purées. What they all have in common is that they will balance out the vegetable dishes. These recipes often include olive oil as a fat, vinegar or lemon as an acid and salt as a flavour enhancer. They will elevate the taste of every dish you cook, and will become your favourite accessories to just about anything you eat. Pick a few recipes to start with and pair them up with your most-often-used veggies, and keep one or two in the fridge, ready for use.

Classic vinaigrette

A good vinaigrette reduces the bitterness of vegetables and makes a salad perfectly balanced between salty, sour, bitter and sweet flavours. The secret lies in the combination of oil and sour, which in its purest form has a 3:1 ratio. That means you add 3 tablespoons of oil for each tablespoon of sour – you can alternate between vinegar, lime or lemon juice. To prevent the oil and sour from separating, you add emulsifiers. Whisking in mustard or balsamic binds the ingredients smoothly together. Try your luck by playing around with the quantities of shallots, garlic and maple syrup.

2 tbsp white wine vinegar, apple cider vinegar or juice of
  ½ lemon
100ml extra virgin olive oil
½ tsp maple syrup (optional)
1 shallot, finely chopped (optional)
1 garlic clove, crushed (optional)
generous pinch of freshly ground black pepper
pinch of sea salt

Whisk together the vinegar, oil, maple syrup, shallot and garlic, if using, and pepper to form a vinaigrette. You could also shake the ingredients together in a small lidded jar. Finally, add salt, to taste.

Classic vinaigrette

French mustard vinaigrette

Balsamic vinaigrette

French mustard vinaigrette

2 tbsp white wine vinegar, apple cider
    vinegar or juice of ½ lemon
1 tsp mustard (preferably Dijon)
1 garlic clove, crushed or finely chopped
1 tbsp freshly chopped herbs (optional)
½ tsp maple syrup (optional)
sea salt and freshly ground black pepper,
    to taste
100ml extra virgin olive oil

It's not the end of the world if the oil
separates, but, to be on the safe side,
first mix all the ingredients except the oil
together in a small bowl and then slowly
whisk in the oil. You could also shake the
ingredients together in a small lidded
jar, just wait until the end to add the oil.
However, often it works to put the oil in
with everything else. Whether you have
a perfect emulsion or not, it will still
taste the same when you pour it over the
vegetables!

Balsamic vinaigrette

2 tbsp balsamic vinegar
1 tsp maple syrup
sea salt and freshly ground pepper, to taste
100ml extra virgin olive oil

First whisk together the balsamic vinegar,
maple syrup, salt and pepper, then
whisk in the oil. Or simply shake all the
ingredients together in a small lidded jar.

Green herb oil

If you have some leftover rocket salad or
herbs, you can use them here. You don't
have to heat the oil but, if you do, it will
get more flavour and keep longer.

200ml extra virgin olive oil
1 bunch of herbs, such as parsley, basil,
    rosemary, rocket salad or dill
sea salt and freshly ground black pepper,
    to taste

Heat the oil in a pan to about 60°C (do
not boil). Roughly chop the herbs and tip
into a blender with the heated oil, salt and
pepper. Blend for 3 minutes.

Vegan pesto

Pesto goes with everything – on a slice of bread, on pizza, in pasta, or spread out over oven-roasted vegetables. While traditional pesto contains Parmesan, vegans like to use toasted cashew nuts and nutritional yeast for flavour.

a generous handful of kale
a generous handful of basil leaves, or the
  whole bunch to be extra generous
½ bunch of parsley
2 garlic cloves
1–2 tbsp nutritional yeast, if you have it
  (see page 23 on nutritional yeast)
200ml extra virgin olive oil
100g toasted cashew nuts
50g pumpkin seeds
zest and juice of 1 lemon
a pinch of sea salt

Roughly blend the kale, herbs and garlic in a food processor. Add the nutritional yeast, oil, nuts and seeds, then blend again. Adjust to the desired consistency with more oil, if needed. Season with lemon and salt. It keeps up to 5 days in the fridge.

Five-spice

4 star anise
2 cinnamon sticks
2 tbsp mustard seeds
2 tbsp coriander seeds
2 tbsp fennel seeds

Toast the spices in a dry frying pan over a high heat for 2–3 minutes, turning once or twice, until fragrant. Crush the spices in a pestle and mortar or blend them in a spice grinder. Store in an airtight container.

Classic
hummus

Beetroot
hummus

Caramelised red onion
hummus

Pea hummus

Classic hummus

Hummus is a filling chickpea purée and a vegan's best friend. It's a great addition to everything you cook, and can work as a substitute for potato, rice, pasta or meat. If you are hungry, a large tablespoon of hummus will balance your blood sugar right away – so you don't stick your hand in the biscuit tin before dinner. Here is the recipe for four different varieties of hummus.

2 x 400g tins of chickpeas, drained
4 tbsp extra virgin olive oil
3 tbsp tahini (sesame paste)
1 garlic clove (lightly toasted in the frying
*   pan, optional)*
2 tsp ground cumin
zest and juice of ½ lemon
pinch of sea salt
freshly ground black pepper, to taste
a pinch of smoked paprika, pumpkin seeds
*   or toasted chickpeas, to serve*

Mix everything in a blender or food processor and season further with more lemon juice, salt and pepper, if desired. Sprinkle paprika, pumpkin seeds or whole toasted chickpeas on top before serving.

Beetroot hummus

Beetroot hummus has a wonderful red colour and a rounder and sweeter flavour than classic hummus. Put 1–2 chopped cooked beetroots into the blender along with the ingredients for classic hummus. Serve with a few small cubes of cooked beetroot on top.

Caramelised red onion hummus

This is my favourite hummus! Cut 1 onion into cubes and finely chop 1–2 garlic cloves. Fry in a tablespoon of olive oil until golden. Set aside a little of the onion to serve and put the rest into the blender along with the ingredients for classic hummus. Top with the reserved fried onions and some whole roasted chickpeas before serving.

Pea hummus

This green variety has a slightly fresher taste due to the addition of mint and peas. Put 200g of frozen peas (thawed quickly in boiling water) and 2 tablespoons of freshly chopped mint leaves into the blender along with the ingredients for classic hummus. Serve with a sprinkle of whole peas on top.

Red cabbage and apple slaw

Coleslaw is a tangy cabbage salad that goes with most dishes, and is a popular side dish to fried or grilled food. The red cabbage gives sweetness and a wonderful colour, and the apples give tartness. Serve with Falafel (see page 134).

1 red cabbage, grated
2 green apples, grated
3 spring onions, finely chopped
1 tbsp apple juice
2 tsp apple cider vinegar
1 tsp Dijon mustard

Put the cabbage into a large bowl. Mix in the apples and spring onions. Add the apple juice, vinegar and mustard and stir together well. Chill in fridge before serving.

Pea purée with hot chilli

This purée is not for wimps! Try it with
Celeriac Steaks (see page 122) – it adds
loads of extra flavour.

2 green chillies
300g frozen peas, thawed
2 tbsp extra virgin olive oil
a pinch of sea salt

Remove the stalks from the chillies and
fry gently in a pan for a few minutes. Place
everything in a blender, or use a hand
blender, and mix to a smooth purée. If you
wish, use 1 tablespoon more of olive oil.

Grilled aubergine purée

A veggie classic! Perfect on a slice of bread or try it with Grilled Cabbage (see page 112).

olive oil
2 aubergines
4 garlic cloves, crushed
½ tsp smoked paprika
juice of 1 lemon
a pinch of sea salt
a pinch of freshly ground black pepper

Rub a little oil on the aubergines and place them in a roasting tin. Add the garlic and drizzle with a little more oil. Bake in the oven at 180°C/160°C fan/gas mark 4 for about 30–40 minutes, or until soft. Scoop the aubergine flesh from the skins into a bowl. Roughly chop, add a drizzle of olive oil and season with the paprika, lemon juice, salt and pepper. Mix well and serve.

Pickled red onions

Amazingly simple. An exciting addition to a slice of bread, and a must on Tacos (see page 128).

150ml water
3 tbsp sugar, preferably coconut sugar if you have it
1 tsp salt
100ml apple cider vinegar
5 slices of fresh root ginger (no need to peel)
1 tsp peppercorns
1 tsp coriander seeds (optional)
2 red onions, thinly sliced into rings

Mix the water, sugar, salt and vinegar in a pan. Bring to the boil. Once the sugar has dissolved, add the ginger, spices and red onions. Remove the pan from the heat and set aside to cool. Fill a clean jar with the mixture, making sure the onions are covered. Store in the fridge for 2–3 weeks.

Vegan mayonnaise

Sriracha dressing

Vegan aioli

Vegan mayonnaise

After hummus, this is the vegan's second best friend. It tastes amazing and is super easy to make. Aquafaba, the liquid from a tin of chickpeas, is an important part of this recipe. Aquafaba varies slightly in thickness depending on the tin it comes from, but try to use a thick and gooey aquafaba.

6 tbsp thick aquafaba
300–500ml extra virgin olive oil
1 tbsp white wine vinegar or juice of
    ½ lemon
1 tbsp Dijon mustard
pinch of white pepper
pinch of salt

nb! Before you start, you need to know that it is important to put the salt in last, after the mayonnaise is finished, because otherwise the mayonnaise will bind together. Also be careful not to use too much oil; start with maximum 400ml and if the mayonnaise does not become thick and creamy, add more.

Put the aquafaba, 400ml olive oil, the vinegar or lemon and the mustard in a tall, narrow container, such as a tall jam jar. Gently blend the mixture using a hand blender for a minute or so. Continue mixing until everything turns white and creamy. If necessary, add more olive oil for the desired thickness. Add a little white pepper and salt to finish. The mayonnaise keeps for 5 days in the fridge.

Vegan aioli

Aioli is thicker in consistency than mayonnaise and has a lovely taste of garlic.

Start with the recipe for vegan mayonnaise. Put 4 tablespoons of vegan mayonnaise in a bowl. Add 1 crushed garlic clove, ½ teaspoon Dijon mustard and 1 teaspoon olive oil, then whisk together.

Sriracha dressing

Sriracha is a strong Thai-inspired chilli sauce made from sun-ripened chillies, vinegar, garlic, sugar and salt. It almost has a kind of rock-star status; abroad, fans of the sauce discuss whether to write it with a big or small 's'. The world-famous sauce is the origin of songs and slogans. In San Francisco, I once bought a T-shirt with: 'I want Sriracha on my Sriracha!'

Put 4 large tablespoons of vegan mayonnaise into a bowl. Stir in 1 teaspoon vegan sriracha until completely mixed and add more to taste.

Tahini dressing

Miso dressing

Mustard dressing

Tahini dressing

Tahini is a blend of sesame seeds that you can buy in all health-food stores and many mainstream supermarkets. This creamy dressing is a nice alternative to a vinaigrette. Try it with Fried Rice with Edamame (see page 142), or in any dish with cauliflower.

2 tbsp tahini
juice of ½ lemon
1 tsp maple syrup (optional)
pinch of ground cumin
generous pinch of sea salt
3 tbsp ice-cold water

Mix everything together in a blender or with a hand blender while adding the water 1 tablespoon at a time until you have a slightly sticky consistency. Keeps for 4 days in the fridge in an airtight container.

Miso dressing

Miso consists of fermented soybeans, rice and grains and comes in the form of a sticky paste. The most common type has a reddish-brown colour, but you can also get a milder white miso. A miso dressing gives you the long-awaited and slightly mysterious umami flavour. Try miso dressing on Fried Rice with Edamame (see page 142).

2 tbsp white miso paste (if you can't find white
    miso, take the one they have in the store)
1 tbsp Dijon mustard
1 tbsp cold water
4 tbsp extra virgin olive oil

Mix everything together with a hand blender. Even easier, you could also shake the ingredients together in a small lidded jar.

Mustard dressing

Mustard adds an extra punch to salads and vegetables. Have you tried mustard-roasted cauliflower? This dressing is made for it! Cover a whole cauliflower head with the dressing, spreading it between the florets. Then follow the same method as for the Whole Roasted Cauliflower with Chipotle (see page 100).

3 tbsp Dijon mustard
2 tbsp apple cider or white wine vinegar
1 garlic clove, crushed
100ml olive oil
pinch of sea salt

Mix everything together in a blender or shake together in a small lidded jar. If the dressing is too thick, use up to 100ml more olive oil. Store in a jar in the fridge and it will keep for several days.

ps. The dressing can set when it gets cold, so remember to take it out in good time before you use it.

Crispy chipotle cashew nuts

Turmeric-roasted peanuts

Fennel-roasted chickpeas

We must have snacks!

Here are three simple and crunchy vegan snacks that are sure to get people excited.

Crispy chipotle cashew nuts

250g cashew nuts
2 tbsp chipotle in adobo sauce
1 tsp fennel seeds
pinch of Ceylon cinnamon
1 tbsp maple syrup
1 tbsp apple cider vinegar
1 tbsp sesame seeds
1 tbsp sea salt

Mix all the ingredients in a bowl and spread out on a baking sheet lined with baking parchment. Place in the oven at 160°C/140°C fan/gas mark 3 for about 15 minutes, or until the nuts are golden and crispy.

Turmeric-roasted peanuts

250g raw unsalted peanuts
3cm piece of fresh root ginger,
    finely chopped
1 tbsp coconut oil
1 tbsp coconut flakes
½ tsp ground turmeric
½ tsp chilli flakes

Mix all the ingredients together in a bowl and spread out on a baking sheet lined with baking parchment. Place in the oven at 160°C/ 140°C fan/gas mark 3 for about 15 minutes, or until the nuts are golden and crispy.

Fennel-roasted chickpeas

2 x 400g tins of chickpeas
2 tbsp olive oil
juice of 1 lemon
2 garlic cloves, crushed
1 tsp ground cumin
1 tsp ground coriander
1 tsp fennel seeds, crushed
1 tsp smoked paprika
1 tsp sea salt

Drain and rinse the chickpeas (keep the aquafaba for your vegan mayonnaise!). Mix all the ingredients in a bowl and spread out on a baking sheet lined with baking parchment. Bake in the oven at 160°C/ 140°C fan/gas mark 3 for about 20–25 minutes, or until the chickpeas are golden and crispy.

diary notes

day **1**	**food**
	today's mood

day **2**	**food**
	today's mood

day **3**	**food**
	today's mood

day **4**	**food**
	today's mood

day **5**	**food**
	today's mood

day **6**	**food**
	today's mood

day **7**	**food**
	today's mood

day 8	**food**
	today's mood 😌 😐 🙁

day 9	**food**
	today's mood 😌 😐 🙁

day 10	**food**
	today's mood 😌 😐 🙁

day 11	**food**
	today's mood 😌 😐 🙁

day 12	**food**
	today's mood 😌 😐 🙁

day 13	**food**
	today's mood 😌 😐 🙁

day 14	**food**
	today's mood 😌 😐 🙁

day **15**	**food**
	today's mood

day **16**	**food**
	today's mood

day **17**	**food**
	today's mood

day **18**	**food**
	today's mood

day **19**	**food**
	today's mood

day **20**	**food**
	today's mood

day **21**	**food**
	today's mood

day **22**	**food**	**today's mood**
day **23**	**food**	**today's mood**
day **24**	**food**	**today's mood**
day **25**	**food**	**today's mood**
day **26**	**food**	**today's mood**
day **27**	**food**	**today's mood**
day **28**	**food**	**today's mood**

index

aioli 157
algae 64–5
animal-rights movies and
    documentaries 75
apples: red cabbage and apple
    slaw 152
aquafaba 22
aubergines: grilled aubergine
    purée 155
avocados 17, 25
    avocado cream 128
    broccoli and avocado wok 116

beans 20, 25, 29, 44, 49
beetroots 17
    beetroot hummus 151
    salt-baked beets 140
Berg, Alexander 15
bitter 14–15
blood sugar 12, 50–1, 88
breakfast 24, 30
broccoli 15, 18, 25, 47
    broccoli and avocado wok 116
    tenderstem broccoli and
        tofu 118
burger: Beyond Meat burger
    70–1
butter 63
butternut squash: red Thai curry
    with butternut squash 106
    roasted butternut squash with
        quinoa 104
    see also pumpkin

cabbage: cabbage salad 110
    grilled cabbage with miso
        dressing 112
    pickled red cabbage 51
    red cabbage and apple slaw
        152
carrots 17
    fried rice with edamame,
        mushrooms and
        carrots 142
    garlic-roasted chickpeas and
        carrots 138
cashew nuts: crispy chipotle
    cashew nuts 161
cauliflower 11
    cauliflower rice with quinoa
        98
    cauliflower risotto 96
    whole roasted cauliflower
        100
celeriac 18
    celeriac steaks with crushed
        edamame 122
cheese 9, 63
chia seeds 21, 29
    chia pudding 30
chickpeas 20, 29, 44, 51
    falafel 134
    fennel-roasted chickpeas 161
    garlic-roasted chickpeas and
        carrots 138
    hummus 151
chipotle cashew nuts 161
coconut milk 23
    golden milk 53
coconut oil 23
cream 63

eating out 34–6
edamame beans 49
    celeriac steaks with crushed
        edamame 122
    fried rice 142
    red lentil dahl 132

falafel 134
fennel: cabbage salad 110
fennel seeds: fennel-roasted
    chickpeas 161
fermentation 66–7, 68
five-spice 149
    tacos with five-spice fried
        sweet potato 128
flaxseeds 21
flexitarians 9, 72
food prepping 40–1
food waste 69, 80
frozen food 42

garlic 18
    garlic-roasted chickpeas and
        carrots 138
gluten 56–7, 59
golden milk 53

health and wellbeing 7, 12, 32–3,
    52–5
herbs 19, 39
    green herb oil 147
hummus 33, 47, 51, 151

iodine 60, 61, 65
iron 60, 61, 65

kale 19
    roasted butternut squash 104
kimchi 66–7
kitchen cabinets 24–6, 38–9, 80
kombucha 66–7

lacto-vegetarians 9
lemon 18
lentils 20, 25, 29, 44, 49
    red lentil dhal 132

mangoes: cabbage salad 110
    mango salsa 128
mayonnaise 157
milk 25, 29, 45, 63
    golden milk 53

minerals 60
miso 23, 67
    grilled cabbage with miso
        dressing 112
    miso dressing 159
mushrooms: fried rice with
        edamame, mushrooms and
        carrots 142
    sweet potatoes with
        chanterelles in herbal
        oil 62
mustard: French mustard
        dressing 147
    mustard dressing 159

nutritional yeast 23, 39
nuts and nut butters 21, 44, 49

oat milk 25, 26
    golden milk 53
oats 21
    overnight oats 30
olive oil 23
    green herb oil 147
omega 3 12, 64–5
onions 17
    caramelised red onion
        hummus 151
    pickled red onions 51, 155
ovo-lacto-vegetarians 9
ovo-vegetarians 9

pasta 27, 36–7
peanuts: turmeric-roasted
        peanuts 161
peas 47
    pea hummus 151
    pea purée with hot chilli 153
peppers 18
pescatarians 9
pesto 149
pomegranate: cabbage salad 110
protein 33, 46–9

pumpkin 19
    see also butternut squash
pumpkin seeds 22, 29

quinoa 20, 47
    cabbage salad 110
    cauliflower rice 98
    roasted butternut squash
        104

rapeseed oil 23
ready meals 59, 70–1
rice 20–1, 25, 44, 45
    fried rice with edamame,
        mushrooms and
        carrots 142
    red Thai curry with butternut
        squash 106

salt 15, 22
salty 14–15
satiety 50
seeds 21–2, 44, 49
sesame seeds 22
shopping 28–9, 40–5, 80
sour 14–15
soy 27
soy sauce 23
spaghetti veganese 37
spices 22
spinach 18
sprouts 19
sriracha dressing 157
stress management 12
sunflower seeds 22
sweet 14–15
sweet potatoes 17
    with chanterelles in herbal oil
        62
    salt-baked and grilled sweet
        potato 126
    tacos with five-spice fried
        sweet potato 128

tahini 23
    tahini dressing 159
tamari 23
tapas 91
tempeh 29, 47
tofu 29, 47, 49
    tenderstem broccoli and tofu
        118
tomatoes 17
    cauliflower rice 98
travelling 34, 82–3
turmeric 53, 54
    turmeric-roasted peanuts
        161

umami 14–15, 66

vegans 8
    celebrities 46, 74, 85
    domino effect 72–3
vegetarians 9
vinaigrettes 146–7
vinegar 23
vitamin B12 33, 60, 61
vitamin D 33, 60, 61

waffles 91
weight control 12–13, 33
wellbeing see health and
        wellbeing
wheat 56–7, 59

yoghurt 29, 63

The right of Laila Madsö to be identified as the author of the work has been asserted
by her in accordance with the Copyright, Designs and Patents Act 1988.

Originally published by Gyldendal Norsk Forlag AS, Oslo in 2020

First published in Great Britain in 2020 by Headline Home
an imprint of Headline Publishing Group

1

Cataloguing in Publication Data is available from the British Library

Hardback ISBN 978 1 4722 7856 2
eISBN 978 1 4722 7857 9

Cover and design: Randi Holth Skarbø
Food styling and chef: Alexander Berg
Photographers: Jim Hensley and Nina Dreyer Hensley
Copy editor: Sophie Elletson
Proofreaders: Margaret Gilbey and Sally Sargeant
Indexer: Caroline Wilding

Printed and bound in Italy by LEGO S.p.A

Headline's policy is to use papers that are natural, renewable and recyclable products and
made from wood grown in sustainable forests. The logging and manufacturing processes
are expected to conform to the environmental regulations of the country of origin.

HEADLINE PUBLISHING GROUP
An Hachette UK Company
Carmelite House
50 Victoria Embankment
London EC4Y 0DZ

www.headline.co.uk
www.hachette.co.uk

thanks

I am grateful to everyone who believes in me and my plant-based mission. My family who, in their different ways, show me love. My husband who shares my passion for all green stuff, even becoming a vegan along the way. My two little girls who support me with their huge appetite for veggies, and their approving compliments at the dinner table.

My mother who trusted my advice to give up dairy products, and who recently reversed her diabetes. My supportive group of girlfriends, many who have done their own 28 days vegan, and some even remaining plant-based happily thereafter.

Special thank yous to the brilliant power-duo photographers Nina Dreyer Hensley and Jim Hensley for taking all the beautiful pictures in this book. Additional special thanks to superb designer Randi Skarbø for her skills and professional work.

Lastly, but most importantly, a giant thank you to the culinary captain, chef Alexander Berg. I am so happy that you, Alexander, one of Norway's top rockstar chefs, joined me in the cooking of this book.

Testimonials from previous meat eaters who have taken on the vegan 28-day challenge

Day 3:
I think Day 3 is very nice text. Just the way it is. I have gone on diet plans before, but this time I noticed that I quickly stopped shopping on autopilot. Admittedly, I go all in now as I try to avoid wheat and grain products as well as meat. I drink a lot of almond drink, but I think it's a little too sweet. Have to try oat milk. Today I was extra wary in the grocery shop :-) That list of additives came in handy. In general, I find it easier to just buy vegetables, not so much ready-made meals. Today I felt a boost of energy!!

Woman, 48 years

Day 9:
My God, this is a breeze! Zero problems! Did a bit of mental work to stay clear of all the traditional foods at our National Day breakfast buffet, but I had prepared lots of vegan dishes, too, so I managed to stay clear of all the meat cuts, herring fish, cheese and cream . . . Missed the fish especially, but yes – this plan is brilliant!!!

Woman, 54 years

Day 10:
Got very inspired today. Have been planning on making beetroot hummus for a long time. I'll test that tomorrow. I got a little scared and wondered if I eat too many seeds? I love sesame seeds and eat them as snacks! Everything is going well, thank you! I notice that my yoga routine is easier when I eat plant-based.

Woman, 23 years

Day 13:
Nice summary of what supplements to take. It's not easy to get a clear picture of this from the wilderness of information online. Today I have cleaned out the kitchen cupboards again and have an eating plan ready for the coming week. Very nice to have the inspiration from the plan to hold on to.

Woman, 39 years

Day 15:
Yes yes yes! I dig this. Here it is! Things I wondered about in the first weeks make perfect sense now. Great recommendation about the omega-3 supplements. Tons of interesting info, good examples and explanations. This one is absolutely super!

Woman, 23 years